E

71

5

Muirhead Library of Philosophy

EDITED BY H. D. LEWIS

LECTURES ON PHILOSOPHY

BY G. E. MOORE

Principia Ethica
Ethics
Philosophical Studies
Some Main Problems of Philosophy
Philosophical Papers
Commonplace Book 1919–1953

LECTURES ON PHILOSOPHY

BY
GEORGE EDWARD MOORE
O.M.

Fellow of Trinity College, Cambridge,
and Emeritus Professor of Philosophy
in the University of Cambridge

EDITED BY
CASIMIR LEWY

Fellow of Trinity College, Cambridge,
and Sidgwick Lecturer in Moral Science
in the University of Cambridge

LONDON : GEORGE ALLEN & UNWIN LTD
NEW YORK : HUMANITIES PRESS INC

248055

PRINTED IN GREAT BRITAIN
in 11 on 12 point Imprint type
BY UNWIN BROTHERS LIMITED
WOKING AND LONDON

EDITOR'S PREFACE

This volume consists of selections from three courses of lectures. The first course was given in the academic year 1925–26, the second in 1928–29, and the third in 1933–34. The first two (entitled "Metaphysics") were intended primarily for Part II of the Moral Sciences Tripos; the last (entitled "Elements of Philosophy") for Part I. (The selections from the second course, which are the most extensive, are printed first.)

The task of editing Moore's lecture-notes was not an easy one. They were not intended for publication and he never revised them. Moreover, each of the three manuscripts consists of a bundle of loose sheets, and in each bundle many sheets are missing altogether and many others are very fragmentary indeed. A great deal of editorial work was therefore necessary in order to produce anything suitable for publication. And I thought that this could be best achieved by omitting those portions of the manuscripts which were so closely connected with the missing or fragmentary ones as to be very largely unintelligible. The only other possibility was to attempt to reconstruct the missing and fragmentary parts. But I could see no way of doing so.

There was another difficulty. Many of the sheets have remarks written in the margins, on the back, and even between the lines of the text itself. It is not always clear where these remarks should be inserted, and I thought it best to indicate the insertions by enclosing them in pointed brackets. Round brackets, on the other hand, are Moore's, except that I have added them in those places where he had obviously left them out by oversight. Lastly, square brackets are used for my own insertions and also for my own footnotes.

I have in general retained Moore's contractions of words, and I have not interfered systematically with his use of quotation marks and italics. This is not uniform, but I do not think that it will cause the reader serious difficulty. I have also interfered as little as possible with Moore's punctuation.

The division into sections and the titles of the sections are my own; but the order in which the sections are arranged is the same as in the manuscripts.

I am very grateful to Mrs G. E. Moore for her advice on a number of questions; to Timothy Moore for his help with proof-reading; and to the Rockefeller Foundation for financial assistance in connexion with the typing of the manuscripts.

C. LEWY

Trinity College
Cambridge
September 1965

CONTENTS

PART I

SELECTIONS FROM A COURSE OF LECTURES
GIVEN IN 1928–29

I

WHAT IS MEANT BY "NATURE"?

What is meant by Nature; & what has philosophy to do with it— what kind of questions about Nature are philosophical, as opposed to scientific, questions.

This term "Nature", with a capital "N", is constantly used in philosophy, as elsewhere, as if we all understood what it meant; but I think it's important for philosophy to attempt to define it.

There are 2 senses, pretty sharply distinguished: a narrower & a wider.

(1) The narrower in wh. Phil. of Nature is opposed to Phil. of Mind—i.e. one in wh. Nature *doesn't* include our minds & mental processes; the sense in wh. Whitehead uses it, when he talks about Nature being closed to Mind; the sense in wh. it is used when we talk of Natural as opp. to Moral Science, & don't include Psych. in the Natural Sciences.

(2) A wider sense in wh. our minds & mental phenomena, all those of living creatures on the earth or anywhere in the material universe, are included in Nature.

⟨It might be thought that in this sense Nature is identical with the Universe; & so *perhaps* it is in extension; but certainly not in intension, since it is possible to hold without contradiction that there are existents which neither are Nature nor fall within it. E.g. the Absolute.⟩

Both these conceptions are important conceptions & neither is at all easy to define.

We're obviously meant to confine ourselves to (1); & (1), with a certain proviso, = the material universe. The proviso is that if, as some Behaviourists & Materialists seem to have held, all our mental processes are, in fact, merely material processes, then we should have to define Nature = all that part of the material universe wh. is *not* mental. I think such views are certainly not true, & in that case Nature simply = the material universe.

(2) in any case needs, I think, to be defined by reference to material universe; it is the material universe & all mental entities that have a certain relation to it.

In any case, the def. of Nature, in our sense, depends on def.

3

of "material universe": either it's identical, or we have to define it as material universe minus whatever is mental in it.

What do we mean by "the material universe"?

Let's consider the matter in this way:

There are two *prima facie* different types of entity, which we certainly consider as forming part of, or included in, the material universe. I mean: physical *things* & physical *events*. I mean by "things" what Johnson calls "continuants" & Whitehead physical objects. The sun, the earth & planets, the stars & nebulae etc. certainly form part of or belong to the material universe. And there is at all events a *prima facie* difference between them & physical *events* during an earthquake, or the eruption of a volcano: which also form part of the material universe. There are, as you know, some philosophers who maintain that continuants are really only a certain sort of event, e.g. Broad, & still others who think they can only be defined in terms of events. And I shall presently discuss this: I don't think it can possibly be true. But even if it is, we can at all events say that both physical continuants & physical events are included in the material universe.

Can we then say that by the material universe we mean the sum of all physical continuants past, present & future, & all physical events past, present & future? All these are included in it: can we say it is their sum, or the class of which they're all members?

The first thing I want to say is that though, in a sense, I think we can, yet in another sense, & perhaps the most obvious one, I think we certainly cannot.

Both by physical things & by physical events, one thing we mean, is things & events of a certain character or quality: & the first thing I want to emphasize is that, if we mean this, we can't say that the material universe means the sum of all such things, because there may be parts of such things which don't belong to the physical universe *at all*.

This is a point which I'm afraid some philosophers might deny, but which seems to me quite clear, & a point that certainly should be considered in philosophy.

Why I say it is this.

When we talk of *the* material universe, I think it's quite plain we always really mean *this* material universe: the material universe, for instance, to which the sun & the earth belong. And *this* material universe does not include necessarily all material things, but only those which have or had or will have a certain positive *real* relation—not merely a relation in respect of *resemblance*—to the sun, or any other object belonging to it which we pick out. You may say the material universe is a *unity* constituted by the fact that not merely all the things within it are of a certain sort, but that there's a certain *real* relation which holds between any 2 of them.

Now there may be, so far as I can see, ever so many continuants which *resemble* physical continuants, & *are* in that sense physical continuants, & yet haven't got this relation to the sun say. I think we certainly don't know that there are any; but it is logically possible that there should be; & to say this is to say that we can't define the material universe simply as the sum of all physical things & events; but only as the sum of all those which have a certain relation to *this* physical event. This is one reason why Nature certainly isn't identical with the whole Universe.

Try to consider what actually happens when you think of Nature.

By "Nature", then, I think, we mean: All the entities which have a certain property.

But what property?

I feel great hesitation as to what I'm going to say; for it's certainly not easy to see for certain: but I can't help thinking that something *like* what I'm going to say is true, & that it contains very important points.

It seems to me that the connotation of the word Nature is almost certainly *different* nearly every time we use the word: though the denotation is always the same: that is to say we are referring to a class of things defined by an immense number of different properties. The only question is then of saying what *sort* of properties they are. *One* class of such properties is the following.

What are we thinking of when we actually think of Nature?

I can't help thinking that we all of us are always thinking of some particular material thing or a number of them—a different one on different occasions, but always *some* particular one or group.

And here I mean by a material thing, a thing wh. is material in the sense in which my body most certainly is so: there is such a sense, *what* it is we shall be engaged in trying to define: but it certainly includes 2 things (a) having shape & size in 3 dimensions, in the sense in which my body *has*—a sense with wh. we are all familiar, though the analysis of it is difficult & (b) continuing to exist for a certain time, in the sense in which my body has done so.

Starting from this, part at least of what we mean by Nature is, I think, this thing together with all those wh. have the property of being related to it in *both* the following ways:

(a) are similar to it in the 2 respects mentioned

(b) are also positively related to it in this respect: that they either have been or will be, or *both* have been and will be, at every moment of their existence, *in the same space* in which it is or was.

The first point I want to insist on is that *both* these things are necessary in order that a material thing may form part of the material Universe or of Nature.

So far as I can see, there *may* be things wh. fulfil the first without the second; & in that case they would not be parts of *the* material Universe or *Nature*.

What I'm insisting on is that Nature does *not* mean merely all those things wh. have a certain intrinsic property: but all those things wh., *besides this*, stand in a certain relation to *this* thing.

Try to think of what you mean by all the things that are *now* parts of Nature, or parts of the Material Universe.

This is, of course, only a part, because things that have been & have ceased to exist, & things that will be (if any will be) will also be parts of nature.

Well, *one* natural way of thinking of it, is, I think, certainly this.

We start from certain things we are *perceiving*, things in this room, our own bodies & their parts, this desk & so on, these are quite certainly *part* of Nature *now*: not mere sense-data: whether these are or are not included in Nature, is to be left over.

But this does not constitute the whole of Nature now: we know that there are, or may be, other things which are also parts of Nature now: we know that is, of certain properties, that *if* there are any things wh. have those properties they also are parts of Nature now.

What properties?

These at least: Things wh. *resemble* our bodies etc. in this respect at least, that they have size & shape in 3 dimensions, in the familiar sense, whatever it is, in which our bodies have

& *also* have one or other of *three* important relations to things we are perceiving:

are either parts of, or in contact with, or at some distance from them.

Part at least of what we mean by Nature *now* is *"Those* things & all those things that satisfy the 2 conditions (a) that they're extended in 3 dimensions (b) that they are in the same *Space* with these."

This may not be *all*, but it is part.

But now, for the past & future.

We don't necessarily include in Nature all the things wh. have been or will be, which are extended in 3 dimensions.

It's only those among them wh. fulfil a condition analagous to (b) —have been or will be in the same Space with *these*.

And the trouble is that to say that A was in the same space in which B is, can't have the same meaning as *is* in the same space in wh. B is.

I said when we think of Nature on any occasion, we have vaguely in our minds a certain property, & what we mean is: "all the entities which possess this property".

I said it's a different property on each different occasion, but the different properties all have the same extension.

And then I went on to try to describe what *sort* of properties they were, by giving an instance of one of the sort.

But I didn't complete this.

I said starting from anything wh. I am now perceiving in the sense in which I'm perceiving my hand, the blackboard, that clock, *part* of what I mean by Nature may be:

This thing, together with all that fulfil the 2 conditions

(a) that they have size & shape in 3 dimensions *in the same sense* in wh. this has it

(b) that they are all of them in the same Space with it = *either* parts of it *or* in contact with it *or* at some distance from it—again, in certain defined senses (= R).

⟨It's possible, as far as I can see, that there may be things existing now, which satisfy (a) but not (b). If so, they are certainly not parts of Nature.⟩

But obviously this isn't all we mean, since things that have ceased to exist, or wh. don't yet exist, did belong to Nature.

B

And such things simply haven't got now to any of the things I'm perceiving now relation (b).

What they do have to those is some relation wh. can be expressed by saying that they *were* in the same space in which *these* are.

Now the analysis of this I don't pretend to give, but I said I thought I could give a criterion = something which is true of all those things & those things only which *were* at any time in the same Space in wh. these are now.

(1) All those things which exist now as parts of Nature & also existed in the past, were at every moment of this past existence in the same Space in which they now are.

(2) All those things which had *at any time* to one of these the relation R were in the same Space in which these are now.

This includes a very great deal; since e.g. the earth & sun & moon & stars exist now & have existed for a very long time in the past: & every extended thing which has at any time had R to any of these is then included in Nature.

(3) But even this is not enough: for Nature *may* have existed (& that it *may* is enough) before *any* of the things wh. exist now did exist, & *may* continue to exist in the future after they have ceased. What do we mean by this supposition?

I think the case may be met by taking instead of R, R_*[1].

But even this is not enough: this only gives us things in Nature; *events* are also certainly in Nature, & this forms part of our conception.

But how are we to define natural or physical events?

I think we can define them as (1) events which have happened, are happening, or will happen *to* natural things or which happened *where* certain physical things were (I'm inclined to think, in opposition to Whitehead, that to say they happened somewhere in physical space is to say something wh. is to be defined in terms of this), & (2) events wh. are *not* mental events, i.e. *not* of a kind such that any event of that kind must be an *experience*.

If you ask for a property which belongs to all physical things (in wide sense) belonging to Nature which exist *now* & *only* to those, the following will, I think, do: namely this desk together

---

[1] $[R_* =$ the ancestral of R. Cf. *Principia Mathematica*, vol. I, 2nd ed., pp. 543 ff.]

with all other things that are either parts of it or in contact with it or at some distance or other from it. (We ought perhaps to add "or share with it a common part" & "of which it is a part": since I'm afraid I'm wanting to use "thing" in a sense in which this desk together with the atmosphere in this room make *one thing*; & therefore also any part of the desk, together with any part of the atmosphere that is in contact with it. It's only if you do say this, you'll be able to say that any drop of water in a glassful of water is one thing.)

Call this relation "U". U is a relation wh. 2 things can have to one another only if they exist at the same time.

I say among physical things wh. exist *now*, it's only those which have U to this desk that belong to Nature. But it seems to me clearly conceivable logically that there may be any number of physical things (in wider sense) wh. *don't* belong to Nature. Perhaps I'm wrong here. Some philosophers would be inclined to ask: *Where* can they be? The answer must be "nowhere", & this it might be said is self-contradictory, since by def. they are extended & must therefore be somewhere. But "nowhere"means nowhere in the *space of nature*, which is equivalent to *not* having U now to this desk. And it seems to me perfectly conceivable that there are whole worlds of physical things, existing now, that haven't got U to this desk.

But obviously there *have* belonged to Nature things wh. neither have now nor ever have had in the past U to this desk— things wh. existed before it existed; & it certainly *may* be the case that there will be such in the future. What is meant by saying of *such* a physical thing that it has belonged or will belong to Nature?

It neither has nor ever has had nor will have U to this desk; & there *may* be things which neither have, have had, nor will have U to *anything* which exists now.

By "has been" when I use it now I mean what has been previously to the present time; yesterday I meant previously to the then present time; tomorrow (if I exist tomorrow) I shall mean past relatively to the *then* present time.

It might be thought this could be avoided by taking a particular date e.g. noon on Oct. 14, 1923, & defining Nature as all the material things & physical events wh. *are* (in a non-temporal sense) either present or past relatively to or future relatively to that date.

In fact, however, I feel doubtful whether there *is* any such non-temporal sense of *are*—whether in fact "has been" is analysable in terms of *is* (non-temporally) at a time previous to this time: & not rather "is" in any non-temporal sense into "either has been, is, or will be". And even if it can be done, we don't do it: we always do know of any date we take whether it is past, present or future, & speak of it as such.

And even if it is we certainly shouldn't get over the difficulty of having *many* different connotations for Nature, since it's quite certain that by no means every time we use it are we referring to the same date.

And it's quite certain we *don't* mean by Nature all things that have (non-temporally) a certain property which doesn't refer to *any* date.

The Natural Sciences do raise & answer (rightly or wrongly) all sorts of questions about Nature, & everybody is agreed that many of these questions, at all events, are not questions of the kind we now call philosophical, although many that are not of this kind used to be so called when Natural Philosophy was used in the same sense in wh. ["science" is now used].

Thus, to give illustrations wh. it's important to bear in mind:

The question of the age of the earth, how long it has existed, whether as implied in the Bible only since about 4000 B.C., or for longer, & how much longer, is certainly *not* a philosophical question: it's no part of the business of philosophy to discuss whether it's true. Though with regard to another question, not very easy to separate from it, viz. whether *Nature* has *always* existed, I think it must be allowed that it is a philosophical question.

Similarly everybody would agree with Wittgenstein, 4.1122[1], that Darwin's Theory of the Origin of Species, including man, has nothing more to do with philosophy than any other hypothesis of Natural Science: & that whatever it *may* have to do with it, it's *not* the business of philosophy to discuss whether it's true or not.

I've taken these because they're *historical* questions about Nature, dealt with by the Natural Sciences; too often people forget that such questions belong to the Sciences as well as generalizations like the Law of Gravitation.

---

[1] [L. Wittgenstein, *Tractatus Logico–Philosophicus* (London, 1922).]

Whether Newton's Law of Gravitation or Einstein's is more nearly correct is again not a philosophical question.

What questions are philosophical?

It's quite clear that the question I've discussed about whether the word "Nature" has a connotation, & if so what it is, *is* a philosophical question: nobody but a philosopher would discuss it: but it isn't about *Nature*, but about the word Nature, or about a certain concept.

I'm going to distinguish 5 questions, wh. must I think be allowed to be philosophical questions about Nature, & wh. seem to me the most important in the sense that they have been most discussed in philosophy.

I'll formulate them as follows:—

(1) Is Nature Real? or is it an appearance, an illusion?

(2) Do we *know* that Nature is real?

(3) If we do, *how* do we know that Nature is real?

(4) What is the analysis of the concepts that occur in the connotation of "Nature"?

(5) Is Nature, in any sense, dependent on "mind"?

II
ARE MATERIAL THINGS REAL?

Is Nature real? or is it a mere appearance or illusion?

I don't intend to discuss this question *fully* now; some of the detailed questions which require to be gone into for a full discussion will, I think, come better later; but I'll try to indicate now what these are, & I think it's desirable now at once to try to give a general idea of what the points are which do arise.

First of all, some of you may think this is a very queer question to raise. It may seem to you that there's no doubt whatever that Nature is real; & that it's not worth while discussing the view that it isn't; that that view is purely fantastic & absurd. And I'm bound to say I agree as to the first & last point: I do think there's no doubt whatever that Nature is real, & I'm afraid I don't really understand how anybody could have come to think that it isn't. But this calls for an explanation: I think I can understand how people should have come to *doubt* whether it is real; though not how they should have come to think it isn't. By thinking that it isn't, I mean something much more than merely doubting whether it is: I mean, what I think we all do mean, thinking that it's really more likely than not that it isn't or even that it's certain that it isn't. A person who doubts whether it is, may quite well think, though he doubts, that it probably is—i.e. that it's more likely than not; that is to say, he will believe that Nature is real, but will only think we don't know for certain that it is. That is to say, his view will be a negative answer to my second question, not to my first: he will be a believer in the reality of Nature, but one who holds that it's not one of the things we know to be true. This difference of attitude, I think, does really exist & is important; & that's why I distinguished my first & second questions. And I think I can understand how people should have come to have this attitude of doubt; but I'm afraid I don't really understand how anybody should have come to think it's really more likely than not or certain that Nature is an illusion: the view does seem to me absurd & fantastic. That is to say, I'm afraid I shall be an unsympathetic critic of such views.

But though I think the view absurd & fantastic, I do think it's worth while discussing it, & trying to see what there is to be said for & against it; because it seems to me that some of the ablest philosophers have really held it, or, in other cases, have held views which implied it, if not it itself. And it seems to me part of the business of Metaphysics to try to face such views. I shall, I'm afraid, do it badly, because I'm an unsympathetic critic, because I do really think the view simply absurd: but at least I can try to explain why I think so.

But now in all this, I've been assuming that the view that Nature is not real has really been held not merely by madmen but by able philosophers, or at least views which imply it. But is that really the case? I think some people would be inclined to doubt whether it is: I think they would be inclined to think that I've merely misunderstood the views of those philosophers to whom I should attribute this view—that in attacking this view, I'm merely attacking a man of straw; & that the view which *I* mean by the view that Nature is real is a view which nobody has ever doubted or disputed. And that sort of misunderstanding is undoubtedly possible in philosophy: philosophers do express their views so obscurely, often using such a technical jargon, that it's very possible to think they mean one thing when after all they mean another. But nevertheless in this particular case, I can't help thinking that I am right.

Now, on the def. I gave of Nature, Nature can't be real, unless physical things are real. If I was right in saying that it is quite conceivable that there are physical things which don't form part of nature, then the prop. that there are real physical things is by no means equivalent to the prop. that Nature is real: on the contrary there might be real physical things, & yet Nature might *not* be real. In order to prove that Nature is real, it is not sufficient to prove that there are physical things: you have also to prove 2 other things; viz. that there are also physical events: & also that there are both physical things & physical events which form part of a system of physical things & events to which this desk, or some other thing or event which belongs to the same system to which this desk belongs, belongs. You will see that this last condition is one which involves rather complicated logical puzzles to think out. But though, in order to prove that Nature *is* real, you'd have to prove all this; in order to prove that Nature is *not*, it would be sufficient to prove that there are no *real physical things*.

For if there aren't, what we mean by Nature certainly isn't real; though, even if there are, it might well be that Nature isn't. And one reason why I think some philosophers have denied or implied denial of reality of Nature is because I think they've really held that physical things aren't real.

Let's consider then this prop.: that physical things are real— that there really are real physical things.

Some philosophers certainly *seem* to have denied it—to have held that it's most likely or even certainly untrue. But have they, perhaps, not meant by these words what I mean by them? I think that the prop. that physical things aren't real—that there aren't really any real physical things is purely fantastic & absurd. But possibly all the philosophers who seem to have held it have meant something different, which isn't.

Now I think there's no doubt *some* have. One has to admit that the words "Physical or material things are real" are ambiguous, & that in 2 respects: different people mean different things by "material things" & different things by "real".

Let me first try to say how *I* understand them, when I say the prop. that they aren't real is absurd.

(1) How I use "material thing" or "physical thing". I think I can give a very clear definition—a definition much clearer than philosophers generally give; but, as you'll see when I give it, it's a queer *sort* of definition, & unsatisfactory in some ways.

It's a def. by examples: i.e. all I can tell you is that I use "material thing" in such a sense that if there are any chairs, or desks, or blackboards, or planets, or human bodies etc. etc., then there certainly *are* material things.

It seems to me that there certainly is *one* proper use of the terms "material thing", "physical object" etc. which is such that a person who says "there are human bodies, but there are no material things" is contradicting himself, just as would be a person who said "There are things which are red, but there are no things which are coloured" or who said "There are greyhounds, but there are no dogs". It seems to me that if a person tells you "Material things aren't real", you would naturally understand him to imply that this book, this hand, this piece of paper aren't real; & would have a right to accuse him of misusing language if he didn't mean something which implies this.

And to say as much as this, does seem to me to be saying something very clear & definite.

Why it's unsatisfactory is for 3 reasons:

(1) it doesn't enable you to settle definitely, with regard to certain kinds of things that can be mentioned, whether they are material things in the required sense or not: e.g. is a rainbow a material thing; is an electron a material thing?

(2) it's possible that there are several *different* senses of "material things" wh. satisfy the given condition, & it doesn't tell you *which* of them is meant: e.g. it's possible there's one sense in wh. *both* a rainbow & all the things I've mentioned *are* & another in which they *are* but a rainbow isn't.

(3) it doesn't mention any property wh. is both necessary & sufficient for being a material thing: it tells you that to be a human body is sufficient, but of course that isn't necessary.

I'm presently going on to enquire under my *fourth question* what it is that's common to all these different kinds of things, which makes us call them "material": it's of course a very difficult job.

But for the present it seems to me my def., in spite of its defects, is sufficient & very clear: for it enables us to know that the sense of "Material things are not real" with which we're concerned is one which does involve that human bodies, desks, blackboards etc. aren't, & hosts of *other* things, with regard to which, *though* I've only given examples, you will have no doubt.

This being how *I* use "material thing", do philosophers ever perhaps use it in a different sense, a sense in which the denial that material things are "real" does *not* entail that my body is not real?

I think some certainly do. There are, I think, 2 other uses, sometimes adopted, such that "There are no material things" does *not* entail "There are no human bodies".

(a) May be illustrated by reference to Berkeley. B. is commonly held to have denied the reality of matter; and so, in a sense, he does. But if you read him carefully you will find he does *not* deny the reality of human bodies, & clouds, & mountains & loaves of bread. On the contrary he insists he holds such things are real. He is careful to say that what he denies is only *matter in the philosophical sense.* By saying so, he of course implies that some philosophers have used matter in such a sense that to deny

matter does not involve denying loaves of bread. And I think
he's right that they have. And in trying to define what the sense
is, he mentions one characteristic which is, I think, often included—that of being independent of perception. This is, of
course, an ambiguous phrase. But if you *do* include it in your
def., then you are using "material thing" in a different sense.
It may *possibly* be true, as B. would have said, that this desk is not
independent of perception.

⟨"This is a desk but is not independent of perception" is *not*
self-contradictory but "This is a desk but is not a material thing"
is.⟩

From the prop. that there are no extended things that are
independent of perception, it certainly does not follow logically
that there are no blackboards. Of course, I believe myself that
blackboards are independent of perception. But I am not using
"material thing" in such a sense that, if they're not, then they're
not material things. I think myself that such a usage is absurd &
unjustifiable. It seems to me a separate question whether material
things are real, & whether they're independent of perception:
that's why I distinguished (1) & (5). But the questions wouldn't
be separate if we included in the meaning of material things,
independent of perception.

This is one meaning of "material things" such that "There
are no material things" does not entail "There are no blackboards": & therefore a different one from mine.

(b) Another, wh. I think occurs, I will illustrate in this way.
There are some philosophers who seem to hold, I will cite
Leibniz & James Ward, who seem to hold that blackboards &
human bodies are really collections of conscious beings—monads.
And there are some who use "material thing" in such a way, that,
if a blackboard is such a collection, then they would say it isn't a
material thing. They include in the def. of "material things"
"not dependent upon mind" in a sense in wh. if a blackboard
was a colony of monads it would be dependent upon mind. This
again is a quite different usage from mine. I don't use "material
thing" in such a sense that in saying that a blackboard is a material
thing I'm saying that it's not a colony of monads. Of course,
I think it isn't: the view that it is seems to me fantastic & absurd.
But not nearly so fantastic & absurd as the view that there are no
material things in *my* sense.

I say: That is a blackboard, *does* entail "that's a material thing" but does *not* entail "that's independent of perception" or "that's not a colony of monads".

I say *my* sense is the right one, & the others are wrong & improper senses; but even if they're right, they're certainly different.

Possibly there are other senses in which "material thing" may be used such that the denial of the reality of "material things" would *not* involve the denial of this blackboard.

But I've said that I'm only concerned with a use in wh. it *does*.

We are considering the expressions "Material things are real" & "Material things are not real"; and I said that different philosophers may possibly use these expressions to convey very different props., & that for 2 different reasons: (1) bec. they use "material things" in different senses, (2) because they use "are real" in different senses.

I pointed out last time what seems to me to be the chief different senses in which "material things" is used: they can be summed up briefly as follows.

(1) Senses such that from "There are human bodies" *by itself* there follows "There are material things": i.e. such that the prop. "There are human bodies, but there are no material things" is self-contradictory.

I intend to use "material things" exclusively in this kind of sense. I feel quite sure I am right in saying that that is *one* proper usage.

But it's worth noting that this assumes there is no corresponding ambiguity in "There are human bodies". I think there isn't. But it's worth noticing that, as Russell has pointed out, "human bodies" is, in a sense, a *vague* term.[1] Suppose that Darwin's view of the descent of man is true. Then there will in the past have been among the ancestors of man creatures with regard to which it would be impossible to say with certainty whether their bodies were *human* bodies or not. If you go far enough back, there will be creatures of whom you *can* say with certainty that their bodies are not human bodies—that they aren't men; & we can say with certainty that ours are. But at some point in our ancestry there

[1] [B. Russell, "On Vagueness". *The Australasian Journal of Psychology and Philosophy*, vol. I, 1923.]

will have been hosts of creatures—if the transition was gradual, as Darwin supposes—with regard to which you couldn't say whether they are or not: R. says, not only you can't say, but they neither are nor aren't: the Law of Excluded Middle doesn't hold for such terms. And the same can be shewn by considering the development of each human body. The ovum can hardly be said to be a human body; at what point in the development of the embryo does it become one? It seems impossible to draw a clear line. And so, if you consider what happens to the body after death. A skeleton is not a human body; but at what point in the process of decay by which a corpse is reduced to a skeleton, does the corpse cease to be a human body? This kind of consideration is, I think, undoubtedly of great philosophical importance, if only one knew what to make of it: something very important about the nature of concepts & the laws of logic does follow from it. But I must confess I'm wholly unable to see *what* follows.

Why I've mentioned it now is because, in spite of it, my way of defining "material things" by reference to human bodies, & other kinds of things with regard to all of wh. the same sort of difficulty occurs, does seem to me really *clear*, with the sort of clearness that is wanted in philosophy. There isn't any ambiguity about the term "human body", in the sense in which there is about "material thing" or "physical object"; although what I've just said shews that in a sense there is an ambiguity. I don't need to try to define to you what's meant by a "human body", as Broad tries to define what's meant by a physical object. It isn't true that philosophers have ever used the term "human body" in different senses.

(2) Senses such that from "There are human bodies" *alone* "There are material things" won't follow; but such that from "There are human bodies which are *independent of perception*", it will follow.

In saying that there are such senses I am, of course, assuming, what is perhaps disputable, that from "This is a human body" there does *not* follow "This is independent of perception": that is to say that the prop. "This is a human body, but is *not* independent of perception", is *not* self-contradictory.

⟨So far as I can see, with regard to all meanings of "independent of perception", this is true.⟩

(3) Senses such that from "There are human bodies" *alone*

"There are material things" won't follow; but such that from "There are human bodies which are *not* systems of monads" it will.

Here again, it may be held that "This is a human body, and is also a system of monads" is a self-contradictory prop. I don't think it is. But if it is then I'm wrong in supposing that there is such a sense as this.

(4) We ought perhaps also to add: senses such that "There are material things" will only follow from "There are human bodies which are neither dependent on perception *nor* systems of monads".

But now let's turn to different uses of "real". This is a frightfully difficult subject.

III

"REAL" AND "IMAGINARY"

What different things may philosophers have meant by denying the reality of matter (assuming we understand what they mean by "matter") i.e. by "material objects aren't real"?

According to me, one thing they have meant is simply: There are no material objects.

And this is the meaning which seems to me absurd & fantastic. But is it clear what this means?

I think it is. Its contradictory is: There are material objects.

But there are, of course, difficulties about its meaning which I will raise later.

But some people would be inclined to argue that "material objects aren't real" *can't ever* properly mean "There are no material objects", for the following reasons.

(1) They might say
"Material objects aren't real" is of the same form as "Lions aren't blue".

And that, if we examine "Lions aren't blue", we find it means "There are lions, & no lion is blue".

Similarly, then, "Material objects aren't real" must mean "There are material objects, but no material object is real".

And obviously, so far from being identical with "There are no material objects", this is incompatible with it.

They maintain, therefore, that any proper sense of "real" must be such that "Material objects aren't real" is quite compatible with "There are material objects":

∴ there is no sense of "real" such that "Material objects aren't real" = There are no material objects.

This kind of argument has I think really been influential in leading people to suppose that there must be some sense of "real" such that "Material objects aren't real" is quite compatible with "There are material objects". This, I think, may partly serve to explain why Bradley insists that appearances *are* & *exist* & yet aren't real. You see, it presents an argument for the view that in order not to be real, a thing must at least *be*: there must *be* lions,

20

if it's to be true that they're not blue. Similarly it might seem that in order *not* to be real, a thing must at least be.

Now as to this argument, I fully admit that there *are* senses of "real" such that "Material objects aren't real" is compatible with There *are* material objects. But what I want to insist on is that there is a sense in which it's not: & why I've used this argument is because it brings out that to say so involves saying that "Material objects aren't real" is *not* of the same form as "Lions are not blue". For I do think that "Lions are not blue" does = "There are lions & no lion is blue".

In support of my contention consider what is meant by: Unicorns aren't real; griffins aren't real; dragons aren't real.

It's quite clear, I think, that in asserting these things we aren't asserting "There are unicorns", "There are griffins", etc.

But

(2) some people might use another argument in favour of the view that "material objects aren't real" can't possibly be properly used = "There are no material objects".

They might say:

Unicorns & dragons are *imaginary* material objects; & since they are, it follows that there really are imaginary things.

But if there's a sense of "real" such that "There are material objects" = "Material objects are real", then it follows that in *that* sense "There are imaginary material objects" must = "Imaginary material objects are real". But there's certainly no sense whatever of "real" in which imaginary material objects are "real".

(Some philosophers have drawn just the opposite conclusion that there is a sense in which imaginary things *are* real.)

Or, put it in another way: if "Material objects aren't real" = There are no material objects; then "Imaginary material objects aren't real" should mean "There are no imaginary material objects": but it certainly doesn't, in any sense, because "There are no imaginary material objects" is false, whereas the other is true.

I think this argument is really puzzling, & I want to try to say how I shall meet it.

I think the expression "There are imaginary material objects" is true, in a sense, & I also agree that there's no sense whatever in which imaginary material objects are real: and I can, therefore, only meet the argument by saying that the way in wh. "There are" is used in "There are imaginary material objects", where this expresses something true, is different from the way in wh. it's used in "There are material objects": & this seems inconsistent with my maintaining that the latter is unambiguous.

I want to maintain, of course, that though, in one sense, "There are imaginary material objects" is true, in another it is false: that though in one sense "There are no imaginary material objects" is false, in another it is true. What's the difference between the 2 senses?

The argument used to prove "There are imaginary material objects" was "Unicorns are so", therefore there must *be*; & I think it's true that unicorns *are*, & also that in a sense this does prove it. We ought to be able to discover the sense by considering in what sense it's true that "Unicorns are imaginary material objects".

Now it's quite plain that this is *not* like "Lions are mammals" where that has existential import: we're not asserting both "There are unicorns" & "There's nothing which is a unicorn & isn't imaginary".

What it seems to me it does mean is this:
"If anything were a unicorn it would be a material thing, but there are no unicorns (where one includes never have been & never will be)".

If there are, or ever have been or will be, any unicorns, then unicorns are not imaginary.

But in what sense does this conjunction justify the prop. that there are imaginary physical things?

It justifies the prop.: There are *properties* such that both (a) anything which had them would be a material thing & (b) nothing has them.

This, then, is the interpretation I offer of "There are imaginary material things" in the sense in which it's true.

The sense in which it's false is that in which it would mean:
"There are things which are both material things & imaginary", i.e. if it were like "There are vertebrate animals".

Our problem is to find senses of "real" such that the prop. "Material things are not real" is compatible with "There are material things".

I've so far given only one sense of "real" & that is such that "Material things are not real" is incompatible with "There are material things", since it is such that Material things are not real = There are no material things.

And it's to be noticed that with this sense of "real", "Material things are not real" does not mean "*All* material things are not real" ⟨nor yet *Some* material things are not real⟩: on the contrary, it's a sense of "real" such that in the expression "*All* material things are not real", "real" couldn't possibly be being used in this sense; we can say it's a sense of "real" such that, for that sense, "All material things are not real" is meaningless.

For consider. A prop. of the form "All material things are not real" is, as is well known, capable of 2 interpretations—the one with existential import & the one without.

The one without is "There's nothing which is both a material thing & real".

The one with is "There are material things, & there's nothing which is both a material thing & real".

But the sense of "real" we've given is such that "Material things are not real" = There's nothing which is a material thing.

And obviously "There's nothing which is a material thing" can't mean the same as "There's nothing which is *both* a material thing *&* real", since this does not entail "There's nothing which is a material thing".

This is another way of bringing out that with this sense of "real", "real" doesn't stand for any conception since: "There's nothing which is *both* a material thing *&* real" can have a meaning only if "real" *does* stand for a conception.

And still more obviously it can't mean the one *with* existential import; & this also would be meaningless with this sense of "real".

And similarly the sense is one with which "*All* material things are real" will have no meaning.

For this will mean either "There's nothing which is both a material thing & not real"

or "There are material things & there's nothing which is both a material thing & not real".

And with our sense of "real" you can't get any meaning for "There's nothing which is not real".

If, therefore, there *is* any sense of "real" in which "*All* material things are not real" has a meaning (whether true or false), it must be different from this.

c

And now consider the following argument to prove that there is such a sense & to point out what it is.

The use of "real" we've so far considered is one in which it occurs in general props. like "Unicorns are not real", "Lions are real".

The use which *this* argument appeals to is one in which it occurs in *singular* props. like "The unicorn in Alice Through the Looking Glass was not real", "The centaur Chiron was not real", "Caliban was not real", "Mr. Pecksniff wasn't real", "Henry VIII was real". It seems to me it's most important to consider these separately.

Aladdin's lamp was a material thing, & Aladdin's lamp was not real

∴. There is at least one thing which is both a material thing & not real.

But if *this* has a meaning, so will "There is nothing which is both a material thing & real".

Therefore, *this* is a sense of "real" different from the one hitherto considered; & such also that "No material things are real" is compatible with "There are material things"; since the former asserts merely "There's nothing which is both a material thing & real" & this is quite compatible with "There is something which is a material thing".

How are you to meet this argument? It may seem to you a mere quibble; & so I think it is; but I'm afraid some philosophers are inclined to take it very seriously.

Both the premisses are true, in a sense.

But the sense is not such that there follows "There is at least one thing wh. is both material & not real".

From "Aladdin's lamp was a material thing" in the sense in which it's true there does *not* follow "There is at least one material thing" since it only means "Aladdin's lamp, *if* it had existed, would have been a material thing".

That is to say, when we say "There are material things" = Some props. of the form "This is a material thing" are true, we don't mean to include props. like "Aladdin's lamp was a material thing", in the sense in which it's true, but only props. like "This desk is a material thing", where the meaning is different, or St. Paul's cathedral is a material thing.

What is the difference?

When we say "Aladdin's lamp was a material thing" we are I

think undoubtedly referring to a certain property, & are saying: If anything had had this property, it would have been a material thing. (It's very difficult to say *what* property.) And obviously this doesn't imply that there is anything wh. has the property, nor therefore that there is any material thing. When I say "This desk is a material thing" I am again referring to a certain property but I am also asserting that there is something wh. has it.

Surely it is obvious that when you say "Aladdin's lamp was a material thing" you're not asserting that there ever was such a thing as Aladdin's lamp? any more than when you assert that Unicorns are material things, you're asserting that there are unicorns.

For this reason this argument doesn't prove that the sense in which "real" occurs in "Aladdin's lamp was not real", is a sense such that in that sense "There are things which are both material & not real" has a meaning: still less that it's a sense such that "All material things are unreal" *both* has a meaning & is compatible with There are material things.

Yet I'm afraid it's an argument which does appeal to some people.

It can be put in another form as follows:

Aladdin's lamp is an imaginary material thing: ∴ there are imaginary material things: but there are imaginary material things entails there are material things: & if so, "All material things are imaginary" must be compatible with "There are material things".

The mistake is in supposing that "There are imaginary material things", in the sense in which it is true, entails "There are material things": it doesn't: it would only do so, if it meant "There are things which are both material & imaginary", which is meaningless with that sense of imaginary wh. occurs in "Aladdin's lamp is imaginary".

There are imaginary material things = There are properties, which belong to nothing, & which are such that, if they belonged to anything, then they would be material.

I'm afraid, however, some people would still persist that in some sense or other there certainly is such a thing as Aladdin's lamp.

They would say: There must be, because it's just one particular, identifiable imaginary thing: you & I & crowds of other people can all think of just that particular imaginary thing, just

as we can of Caliban & Ariel & Mr. Pecksniff. What on earth can
be meant by saying that we all now are just thinking of Aladdin's
lamp—that it is an object to all of us, if there *is* no such thing?
Of course it's unreal, but it has *being*, & it is material: & hence
from the fact that it is material, it does really follow that there is
at least one material thing.

The point here is a different one from the one I raise explicitly
in *Phil. Studies*, p. 217[1], when I try to explain what must be true
of me, if it's to be true of me at a particular time that I am thinking
of a unicorn. What I say there is true so far as it goes: particularly
of course the fundamental point that "S is thinking of a unicorn"
does *not* mean There is something of wh. it's true both that it is a
unicorn & that S is thinking of it: it's not true that the fact that S
is thinking of a unicorn proves that there is at least one unicorn:
as, if it were true that I was shooting a unicorn, it would be true
that there was: S is shooting a unicorn *does* = There's something
of which it's true both that it is a unicorn & that S is shooting it.
It's also true, I think, so far as it goes, that in order that it may be
true that I am thinking of a unicorn, I must (1) be thinking of
some property, such that, if anything had that property, it would
be a unicorn & (2) conceiving the hypothesis that there is something wh. has that property. But this though it's necessary is
certainly not *sufficient* in order that it should be true that I am
thinking of a particular unicorn: for it is something wh. happens
when I am merely conceiving the hypothesis that *there are unicorns*,
wh. is not the same thing as thinking of a *particular unicorn*. But
I can do this. I can think of the unicorn in Alice Through the
Looking Glass: you & I can both think of the same particular
unicorn. What more am I doing? It is natural here to think of
Russell's statement that "Apollo" means "*the* object having such
& such properties"[2], i.e. as he elsewhere puts it that it is "a
definite description": so that to conceive any hypothesis with
regard to Apollo, e.g. that he was brother of Artemis, is to conceive
with regard to some property or collection of properties, ϕ,
"There's a thing which has ϕ, which alone has ϕ, & wh. is
brother of Artemis". And this is actually offered by R. as an
explanation of how it can be true that Apollo isn't real: he says

[1] [G. E. Moore, *Philosophical Studies* (London, 1922).]
[2] [A. N. Whitehead and B. Russell, *Principia Mathematica*, vol. I, 2nd ed.
(Cambridge, 1925), p. 31.]

that Apollo doesn't exist is of the form $\sim$ E ! $(\imath x)(\phi x)$. It would seem to follow that in his view, whenever I think of a particular imaginary thing, I must be conceiving with regard to some property which in fact belongs to nothing, not merely that it does belong to something, but *that it belongs only to one thing*. Thus in order to be thinking of the unicorn in Alice Through the Looking Glass, I must on his view, so far as I can see, be conceiving, with regard to some property wh. belongs to nothing, that there's a thing which is the only thing which has it & which is also a unicorn. Now I think this *may* be correct, though I very much doubt whether it is. But it doesn't explain how you & I can both be thinking of the same imaginary thing. The explanation which he gives of what happens when you & I both think of the same *real* thing, is that I know with regard to a certain property ϕ, that it belongs to one thing only, & you know with regard to another property χ that it belongs to one thing only; & we shall then be thinking of the same thing if χ & ϕ do in fact both belong to the same thing. Thus, e.g., you may think of Scott as the author of Marmion & I as the author of Waverley, & we shall both be thinking of the same person, because Scott is both the only person who wrote Waverley & the only person who wrote Marmion. R. insists strongly, & I think undoubtedly rightly, that if we call the property which belongs to Scott only, by wh. I think of him on a particular occasion, the *description* by wh. I think of him, & that by which you think of him the *description* by which you think of him, no 2 people ever think of the same real thing by the same description. (Pp. 86–7). [1] It's convenient to use "description" in this sense = McTaggart's exclusive descr. It's true you & I may both think of Scott as the author of Marmion; but even then we're not really thinking of him by the same description: for we both know Marmion only by d., & the d. by wh. I know it is different from that by wh. you know it. But now, suppose that when we think of particular imaginary things, we are, as he seems to suggest, thinking with regard to some property that it belongs to one thing only. There is no reason whatever to think that when 2 people both think of the same particular imaginary thing, the property with regard to which they are thinking that it belongs to only one thing is the *same* in each case. On the contrary there are the same reasons for supposing they will always be different.

[1] [B. Russell, *The Problems of Philosophy* (London, 1912).]

I had begun discussing what it is that happens when 2 different people both think of the *same* imaginary object: as does in fact constantly happen, whenever 2 people think of any famous fictitious thing or person, such as Aladdin's lamp, or Ariel, or Caliban, or Apollo, or the Centaur Chiron, or Mr. Pecksniff. The reason for discussing this being that the fact that we can all think of the same imaginary object may easily seem to be inconsistent with the view which I want to take, & which seems to me to be obviously true, that there *are* no imaginary objects. If there *is* no such thing as Aladdin's lamp, how can you & I both think of *it*? This argument, I think, is probably one of those which influence people who say There certainly *is* such a thing, but it is unreal: or it's a thing which has *being*, but not *existence*. This view, which is a very common one, seems to me to be quite certainly wrong; and I don't think it's possible to understand the most important usages of the words "real" & "unreal", until you see that it is wrong & why it is wrong. But if you're going to say that it *is* wrong, you ought to be prepared to give some account of what the sense is, in which, if it is wrong, 2 different people can think of the *same* imaginary thing. I've never seen any such account & I think it's puzzling; but I think it's a question that's eminently worth considering. I want what I say about it to be at all events *clear*, whether it's right or wrong.

I said that it's natural to think of R.'s theory of descriptions as giving some clue to the question: indeed he does actually offer it as explaining how it is that we can truly say that Apollo is unreal, when there is no such thing as Apollo. He even goes so far as to say that "Apollo is unreal" is a prop. of the form $\sim E!(\imath x)(\phi x)$. (*Principia*, vol. I, 2nd ed., 66 & 67.)

I'm going presently to give 2 separate & distinct reasons for saying that this is a mistake: I think R. is making 2 mistakes in saying it. But so far as I know, he has nowhere tried to explain how you & I can *both* think of Apollo; & the first thing I want to shew, is that even if he were right on the point just mentioned, there are difficulties about this. And in order to bring this out it's necessary to compare what happens in this case with what happens when you & I both think of the same real person, e.g. Julius Caesar or Bismarck.

Now on this point R. does seem to me to have given a perfectly satisfactory account. I think he's the first person in the whole history of philosophy who has done so. His theory of descriptions was perfectly new, & made clear for the first time things about which everybody had gone wrong. Lots of people still don't understand it; but it seems to me eminently worth understanding. I said last time that according to him, when you & I both think of Julius Caesar, what happens is this. I have before my mind some property or other, with regard to which I *know* that it belongs to one thing & only to one thing, & of which also it is in fact true that it's a property which belonged to J.C. & to no one else ⟨*though I don't know this*⟩. Let's call the property which I have before my mind ϕ—it might be that of having written the De bello Gallico, or having been murdered in the Senate House at Rome by Brutus or any of hosts of others—any property (it might be a conjunction of properties) which did in fact belong to J.C. & to no one else, would do. It's convenient to call such properties, as McT. does, "exclusive descriptions": ϕ is an exclusive descr. if & only if it is a property which belongs to one thing & *one thing only*; & it is an exclusive descr. *of* Julius Caesar, if it belongs to J.C. & to no one else. Well, then, when you & I both think of Julius C., I have before my mind some property of which it's true that (1) I know with regard to it that it belongs to one thing & one thing only & (2) also true (though I *don't* know this) that it does belong to J.C. & no one else. Call the property, ϕ. Then R. says that I am knowing to be true the prop. E ! $(\imath x)(\phi x)$—that is merely his way of writing "ϕ belongs to one thing & to one thing only". He says that if (1) I know this with regard to ϕ, (2) ϕ does belong to J.C. & (3) I *don't* know that ϕ belongs to J.C., then "I have merely descriptive knowledge of J.C." & he holds that in fact none of us ever does know of any property that it belongs to J.C., i.e. that we all have merely descr. knowledge of him. Well, then, when you & I both think of him, I'm knowing with regard to ϕ, E ! $(\imath x)(\phi x)$, & you'll be knowing with regard to some *other* property, χ, which also is an exclusive description of J.C. though *you* don't know that, E ! $(\imath x)(\chi x)$. As I said last time, he insists, as I think with obvious truth, that the exclusive d. with regard to which I know this, will always be different from that with regard to which you know it. Even if we both happen to be thinking of him as the author of the De bello Gallico, the description will be different bec. we know this only by description & by different ones. What, then, is the explanation of what's meant by saying that nevertheless we're both thinking of the same person? Simply that the exclusive descr. with regard to which I'm knowing that it belongs to only one thing does *in fact* belong to the same thing as that with regard to wh. you know this. I think this explanation is obviously right, & completely satisfactory. The only queer thing about it is the assertion that I *don't* know that J.C. was the author of the De bello Gallico: of course in a sense I do, but the sense in wh. I do, is that of knowing with regard to 2 different exclusive descrs. that they both belong to the same thing & are both exclusive descriptions.

But now let's ask what happens when we both think of Apollo. Let's suppose R. is right (I think he's wrong) that we are each conceiving with regard to some property the hypothesis that it *belongs to one thing only* ⟨i.e. are conceiving the hypothesis that it is an exclusive descr.⟩. If, as he & I are supposing, there is no such thing as Apollo, the property with regard to which I conceive this hypothesis won't be an exclusive descr. *of* Apollo, bec. if there's no such thing as Apollo no property can belong to him at all: of course it might possibly be an exclusive descr. of something else, but also quite possibly it may not be an exclusive descr. of anything, nor even a descr. of anything: it is *ex hypothesi* a property with regard to which I am conceiving the hypothesis that it is an exclusive descr., but it doesn't follow that it *is* in fact an exclusive descr., nor that it belongs to anything at all, & even if it *does*, *ex hypothesi* on our view of what's meant by saying that Apollo is imaginary, it won't belong to him, because there's no such person for it to belong to. But though thus there's no reason whatever to say that you & I will both be conceiving with regard to some *exclusive descr.* that it belongs to one thing only, there's just as much reason as before to suppose that the property with regard to wh. I'm conceiving that it is an exclusive descr. will be different from that with regard to wh. you are. If you & I never think of Julius Caesar by the same exclusive descr., it's quite certain that the properties by wh. we think of Apollo won't be the same either. But if so, what on earth can be meant by saying that nevertheless we're both thinking of the *same* imaginary object?

It can't possibly be, as in the case of Julius Caesar, that they both do belong to Apollo: bec., on our view that there's no such person as Apollo, nothing can belong to him. Obviously some other account must be given of what's meant by saying that when I conceive with regard to one property ϕ, that it belongs to one thing only, & you with regard to another, χ, that it belongs to one thing only, we are nevertheless thinking of the *same* imaginary object. It must be because ϕ & χ are *somehow* related; but how? I think it may be partly because people have felt obscurely that the relation must consist in their both being exclusive descrs. of the same object, that they have felt that there must *be* such an object as Apollo, though he isn't real: they would say ϕ & χ must really be descriptions which apply to Apollo & Apollo only, else it wouldn't be *Apollo* we were both thinking of. I've seen the objection put in this way. On your view, they say, Apollo, & Aladdin's lamp, & the Centaur Chiron, & Ariel are each of them just *nothing*. But if each of them were just nothing, they would all be the same. But they're *not* the same, & therefore they must have different properties. And obviously what requires to be shewn to answer this is just what is meant by saying that when I conceive of one property ϕ that it belongs to only one thing & you of another χ that it belongs to only one thing, we are nevertheless conceiving the *same* imaginary object. What *kind* of relation must hold between ϕ & χ, in order that this may be so? So soon as we see that this question remains to be answered, even if we do say that I am in fact conceiving with regard to one property ϕ that it belongs to only one thing, & you with regard to another that it belongs to only one thing, it becomes obvious, I think, that the hypothesis that we are doing this doesn't help us at all. Why shouldn't it be the case that we're not? that we're not thinking with regard to any properties that they belong *only* to one thing? We may equally well be able to give an account of what relation between the properties it is wh. makes us say that we're both thinking of the same imaginary object, whether the properties are properties with regard to wh. we are conceiving that they belong to *something*, or whether we are conceiving that they belong *only* to one thing. I don't think, therefore, that there's any reason to accept R.'s suggestion that when we think of Apollo we are thinking with regard to any property that it belongs *only to one thing*: & I shall try to give positive reasons for thinking that we're not. And even if we were, I think he would still be mistaken in saying that "Apollo is a fiction" |is of the form $\sim E!\ (\imath x)(\phi x)$, for this reason. It seems to me quite plain that when we say these

things are fictions, what we are saying is, with regard to some
property or other, that *nothing* has it. But $\sim$ E! $(\imath x)(\phi x)$ does
not say with regard to ϕ that *nothing* has it, but only that it's *not*
the case that only one thing has it. Thus R. is asking us to believe
that when we say Apollo is a fiction, we're only saying with
regard to the properties mentioned in the Classical Dict. under
Apollo, that it's not true that only *one* person possessed them all,
& are leaving it perfectly open that there may have been *several*
who did. Or that when we say that there was no such person as
the author of Slawkenburgius on noses, we are only denying that
"Slawkenburgius on noses" was the work of one man only, &
are leaving it a perfectly open question whether it wasn't written
by several persons.[1] I think there's obviously something wrong
here. In all these cases we're obviously saying of some property
or other that *nothing whatever* possessed it: we're not leaving
open the possibility that, though there wasn't only *one* thing
which did, yet there may have been several. And this is shewn,
I think, by the extremely careless way in wh. R. introduces his
statement. He is then talking of the prop. "the round square
does not exist" (a prop., by the way, which nobody would think
of making; & wh. has no meaning). He says we may substitute
"It's false that there is an object x which is both round & square".
This gives us there are no *round squares*.

But now what does actually happen when 2 people both think
of the same imaginary object? In order to answer this question,
the first thing necessary is to consider what happens when a
person tells you a fairy-tale, or any other fictitious story for the
first time. Take the simplest possible case, such as the parable of
the Good Samaritan in the N.T., or as J. takes (I. 85)[2], the story
of Jack & the Beanstalk—only he tells it quite wrong: J. is talking
about the difference between what he calls the Introductory
Indef. article & the Alternative Indef. He says there's an important difference between "A man must have been in this room" &
"Once upon a time there was a boy who bought a beanstalk":
he says the first means "Some man or other", & the second means
"*a certain* boy" (p. 85). *What* the difference is, he never tells us:
I don't believe there is any. But let's take Luke 10.30: "A certain
man was going down from Jerusalem to Jericho; & he fell among

---

[1] [*Principia*, 2nd ed., vol. I, p. 68.]
[2] [W. E. Johnson, *Logic*, Part I (Cambridge, 1921).]

robbers, which both stripped him & beat him & departed, leaving him half dead". What happens when you hear this? So far as I can see simply & solely that you are led to conceive with regard to a certain property that *someone or other* had it. You don't need to conceive with regard to any whatever that *only* one man had it. ⟨You're not thinking: There was *only* one; but merely "There was some or other" & *failing* to think "There were several".⟩ Obviously there may have been many men to whom this really happened. Yet, if you understand the story, you will have conceived the same imaginary person as the man who tells it to you. It doesn't matter that in this case no proper name is given to the person. A modern novelist would be apt to begin his story not in this simple way, but by saying: "Mr. Smith was going down etc.," as if you knew who Mr. Smith was. But, of course, you don't. What actually happens is merely that you're led to conceive the hypothesis that there was *someone or other* called Mr. Smith to whom certain things happened. What then is necessary, in order that you should be said to have been thinking of the *same* imaginary person as the man who tells the story? Obviously the property with regard to wh. you conceive the hypothesis must resemble in a certain degree the one with regard to which he does. But this though necessary, is not sufficient. A person might independently think of the same story, & yet not be thinking of the same imaginary person. What's essential is simply that *your* conception of the hypothesis with regard to ϕ should have been caused by *his* conception of the hypothesis with regard to χ. The relation wh. must hold between ϕ & χ in order that you in conceiving "Something or other had ϕ", may be thinking of the *same* imaginary person as he in thinking "Something or other had χ", is I think simply that there must be a *causal* relation between your conceiving of the hypothesis on that occasion & his. Of course the *causal* relation needn't be that the one caused the other. It may be that *both* were indirectly caused by the *conceiving* on the part of the person who first told the story. When we both think of Aladdin's lamp, that is because your conception & my conception were both derived from one & the same original one.

In the simplest case, in which a person tells you a story about an imaginary person whom he has invented, he will be conceiving with regard to some property, ϕ, the hypothesis that there was somebody or other who had ϕ, & you will be conceiving with regard to a different property, χ, the hypothesis that there was somebody or other who had χ. ϕ & χ will be similar, in the sense that if there is or had been anything wh. had ϕ & anything wh. had χ, everything which has ϕ *is* similar to everything which has χ, *or* anything wh. had had ϕ would have been similar to anything which had had χ; and in addition to that, what makes you say that you will be thinking of the same imaginary person as A, is according to me simply & solely that your conception of the hypothesis that there was somebody or other who had χ was *caused by* A's conception of the hypothesis that there was somebody or other who had ϕ or rather caused in the particular way in which when you think of a story because somebody else tells it to you, your thinking of it is so caused. Thus the *relation* between the properties ϕ & χ, wh., as I said, there must be, in order that you may both be said to be thinking of the *same* imaginary object, is only partly a direct relation (that of similarity) between ϕ & χ, it is partly an indirect relation constituted by the fact that your conceiving on that particular occasion of the hypothesis that there is a χ is caused in a certain manner by his thinking on that occasion of the hypothesis that there is a ϕ. It seems to me certain that this causal relation must be involved in what we mean, because it is certainly possible, in simple cases, that 2 different people should both invent an imaginary character, such that the resemblance between the ϕ & χ they are thinking of should be quite as great as when you conceive a character wh. someone else has invented, & in such a case we should not say that the character A invented was the same, but only similar to, the character invented by B. We make this distinction between thinking of the same imaginary person, & merely thinking of similar ones, just as we make the distinction between thinking of the same real person & thinking only of a similar one. Only the account of what the difference is, is quite different in the 2 cases.

This account can easily be extended to more complicated cases like our all thinking *now* of Aladdin's lamp. In the case of every imaginary object, there must have been somebody who was the first person who invented it; & when we say that a number of different people are all thinking of the same, what we mean is merely that there was *one* conception of a similar hypothesis such that all of their conceptions were *causally derived* in this particular way, however indirectly, from that one. ⟨Suppose we call the original relation R, the relation wanted is R_*.⟩ Thus we're all thinking of Aladdin's lamp, if we are, because our various conceptions are all derived from a common source—the conception of the original author of the story in the Arabian Nights.

There remains the question what is meant by saying that it's an imaginary or unreal object we're all thinking of. And here I think the consideration of a case like the parable of the Good Samaritan is important. I pointed out there that it may quite well have been the case that there really were many men who went from Jerusalem to Jericho & fell among thieves: not only so, there might quite well have been several of whom the whole story was true. In saying then that the man is an imaginary one, we are not necessarily saying of the character, ϕ, with regard to wh. we conceive that there was something which had it, that *nothing* had that. What we are saying in such a case is, I think, something about the original author of the story: I don't mean that we know who he was; but we know that there was an original author: *what* we are saying is that the original author was not telling the story about a real person; or to put it in another way: we are saying: The conception from which this conception of mine was originally causally derived was not a conception of the form: *This* person went down from Jerusalem to Jericho & fell among thieves, but merely of the form: Some person or other did. That is to say we have to refer to the perfectly obvious & familiar distinction between a fictitious story about a real person & a fictitious story about an imaginary one. Shakespeare represents Richard III as saying ever so many things which no doubt he never said; but nevertheless his play in this case is about a real person R. III, in a sense in which what he tells of Ariel & Caliban is not told of real persons. In order that you should tell a fictitious story about a *real* person, it seems to me to be necessary that you should actually *know* the real person by description in R.'s sense, i.e. there's some description or other, which did in fact belong to him, with regard to wh. you *know* that it is an exclusive descr.: & when you proceed to conceive a fictitious story about him (which you may or may not believe) what happens, supposing ϕ is the description by wh. you know him, & χ the property which you conceive of him as having but wh. he hasn't really got, is that you're conceiving a prop. of the form $(\exists c) : \phi c : x \neq c$. $\supset_x . \sim \phi x : \chi c$, where the first part is something which you *know*, although the whole prop. is something wh. you merely conceive (or perhaps believe too). When, however, you invent a story about an imaginary person, what you are doing is simply to conceive an hypothesis of the form $(\exists c) . \phi c . \chi c$, & *not* to think that there are many such: where no part of the prop. is of the form $(\exists c) : \phi c : x \neq c . \supset_x . \sim \phi x$.

It seems to me then that the full def. of: A & B are thinking of the same imaginary person is simply this: A is thinking of an hypothesis of the form $(\exists c) . \phi c$, & B of an hypothesis of the form $(\exists c) . \chi c$; ϕ & χ are similar; either A's conception of this hypothesis was causally derived from B's of his, *or* vice versa, *or* there is some conception of the same form from which both were ultimately derived: & the conception from wh. one or the other or both were originally derived was *not* of the form $(\exists c) : \phi c : x \neq c . \supset_x . \sim \phi x : \chi c$, where the first part was *known* by the person who formed it.

I said you are saying of some property or other that *nothing* had it; &, on this view, the property of which you're asserting this is that of being a person about whom the original teller of the story was telling it: you are saying that there is nobody of whom it is true that the original teller was telling the story about that person in the sense defined.

And with this meaning of "Apollo is imaginary", it's clear that this assertion is identical with saying that Apollo was not *a historical personage* ⟨in just the sense in which it is discussed whether Agamemnon or Abraham were historical personages⟩. And there may perhaps be some doubt about this: it is just possible that the original person from whom the conception of Apollo was derived, was telling some story about a real person, whom he knew to be real, & perhaps even believing it.

We have, therefore, I think, possibly to recognise *another* sense in wh. we may say "Apollo is unreal", i.e. one in which we are saying with regard to a set of properties, with regard to which, in thinking of Apollo, we are conceiving that someone had them, simply that no-one ever had them. I think we must recognise these 2 different possible meanings of "Apollo is imaginary, or unreal". But whichever you take, the meaning of "we're both thinking of the same imaginary object" will be the same.

I hope I've now made my view clear. To return, for a moment, to the 2 views I have criticised—R.'s & Johnson's.

The point I insisted on as ag. R. is that, in believing that Apollo is unreal, I am not believing any prop. of the form $\sim E \,!\, (\imath x)(\phi x)$. There are 2 reasons for saying this: (1) that I certainly *am* believing a prop. of the form $\sim (\exists x) \,.\, \phi x$ & (2) that, if this were true, in thinking of Apollo I should be conceiving a prop. of the form $E \,!\, (\imath x)(\phi x)$, whereas, so far as I can see, I need only be conceiving one of the form $(\exists x) \,.\, \phi x$, though I must *not* be thinking $(\exists x, y) \,.\, \phi x \,.\, \phi y$.

As for Johnson, I said when I conceive "A certain man went down . . ." I am conceiving neither more nor less than what might be expressed by "Some man or other".

But now to return to the point from which I started—the meanings of "real" & "unreal".

I said it might be suggested that the meaning of "unreal" which occurs in "Aladdin's lamp is unreal" was different from that which occurs in "Unicorns are unreal", & that that meaning, unlike the other, was (1) such that "*All* material things are unreal" would have a meaning & (2) would be consistent with "There are material things".

Now, if what I've said is true, this meaning of "unreal" is just like the meaning which occurs in "Unicorns are unreal", in respect of the fact that in both cases we are merely asserting with regard to some property or other that there is nothing which has it—that it belongs to nothing. And this meaning is such that in a sentence of the form "There are things which are unreal", "unreal" can't possibly have the same sense. But it's only with a meaning of "unreal" such that "There are unreal things" would have a meaning, that "*All* material things are unreal" could have one; $\therefore$ this doesn't give a sense in which that has a meaning.

Of the corresponding sense of "real", as in "The author of Waverley is real", it is also evident that it doesn't give a sense in which "There are things that are real" has any meaning. And here the meaning of "real" is certainly different from what it is in "Horns are real": the difference being that you are in the one asserting of some property that it applies *only* to one thing, whereas [in] the other only [that it] *applies to something*.

It is because this is the corresponding sense of "real" that R. thought "Apollo is unreal" $= \sim E!(\imath x)(\phi x)$.

I went into this bec. I thought it might be tried to shew that this was a sense of "unreal" such that the prop.

(2) "There are things which are both (1) material objects & (2) are unreal" was actually true

by saying that this follows from

(1) "Aladdin's lamp is both (1) a material object & (2) unreal".

It's very easy to think the argument is a good one; because it looks exactly like

"This is a swan & is not white"

∴ "There are things which are both swans & not white"

which is in fact a perfectly valid argument; & bec. (1) is in a sense true; & I don't think most philosophers have in fact been conscious of the difference between the 2 cases.

The difference is that (1) would only yield (2), if "Aladdin's lamp is a material object" were true in a sense wh. yielded "There are material objects": but obviously it isn't since it only = "If Aladdin's lamp existed, it would be", from which you can't infer "There are material objects". It isn't true if you take it to mean "There is something wh. both is Aladdin's lamp & a material object".

And I went into the argument I have gone into, bec. I said people might be tempted to argue "There is something wh. both is Aladdin's lamp & a material object" from the argument that we all can think of Aladdin's lamp.

I don't know if I've persuaded you: I wish I could make it clearer: but the point seems to me of fundamental importance in bringing out the extreme difference between "Aladdin's lamp is unreal" & "This swan is not white" & therefore between "There are unreal things" & "There are things wh. are not white".

I say that with that sense of "unreal" in wh. "Aladdin's lamp is unreal" is true, "There are unreal things" is meaningless.

But now I want to consider another different sort of case, of singular props. in which "real" & "unreal" can occur; bec. it might be thought that here we *have* a meaning such that "All material objects are unreal" has a meaning & is consistent with "There are material things".

There certainly seems some meaning in "This desk is real"; but what?

Let us try to find out by considering what could be meant by "This desk is unreal".

It's quite easy to see by considering a case of hallucination. Suppose a person in hallucination is seeing snakes—unreal snakes. He can pick out a particular imaginary snake & say with regard to it (if he knows he is under an hallucination) That is unreal; & so when I ask: Is this desk unreal? I may be asking whether I am under an hallucination or not.

What is meant here?

I think it's quite easy to see. The person under hallucination is speaking of a particular sense-impression which he has, & is saying of it "This is not an impression of a physical object" *at all*. ⟨This impression is *not* of a snake; or *not* of a material object; ∴ it's not true "This is a snake".⟩ And what I mean by "This desk is real" is similarly "This impression is *of* a physical object". The sense is the same with regard to a sound when we wonder whether it is subjective or objective: we mean is it *of* a physical event or not? What the *of a physical object* means we shall presently consider.

When I say "This desk is real" I am saying "This impression *is of a physical object*"; but the impression isn't the desk, nor does "is real" mean is of a physical object.

Here, therefore, again "real" doesn't stand for any character wh. belongs to physical objects; & if the impression really is of a physical object, the statement "this is unreal" is always false.

We can't then in this way find a property meant by "real" such that there might be physical objects which don't possess it.

But

It might be said this isn't *all* I mean by this desk is real. And I'm inclined to think there *may* be something more.

This seems to me terribly difficult.

Consider first this point.

Suppose there are material things. Mustn't there in that case be a collection of which you can speak as "all the material things *there are*"? This will have no meaning whatever, with the meaning we've given to "there are". Yet it seems as if we meant, all the material things *that have* being. This is what McT. is supposing when he says "reality" is an ultimate notion.

D

Now it may be said this is a mere mistake. That all the material things *there are* simply = all material things: and that we imagine there's a difference, simply because of the inveterate mistake of supposing that imaginary material things *are* material things: that there are 2 classes of material things, imaginary ones & real ones, just as there are 2 classes of animals, birds & mammals.

But there's one reason which makes me think that it may possibly not be a mistake: that there's a sense of "real" such that "Every material thing is real" has a meaning & is true.

The reason is this. Consider the prop. that this desk is real or exists. On the interpretation I've just given this means merely that this impression of mine is an impression *of* a physical thing. And to say that it isn't means merely that it's *not* of a physical thing. But isn't there another way in wh. it might have failed to be true: namely if this impression of mine hadn't existed? Isn't there some sense in supposing that there might have been a universe in wh. this impression simply didn't exist? I can't help supposing there is. But if so, we get a new sense of "real". If it *might* have been the case that this impression didn't exist, there must be some sense in saying that it *does* exist. Only, of course, we mustn't suppose that, if it hadn't existed, there would still have been such a thing, & it would have had the property of not existing: so that this gives us no sense in which it can be true of anything with regard to which we can actually make a proposition, in the sense of "make a prop. about" in wh. you can make a prop. only about something with which you're acquainted, that that thing *is* unreal. Anything about which we can make a proposition in this sense, must *be* real; since if it weren't we shouldn't be able to make a prop. about it. If this impression hadn't existed, it would have been impossible for any one to make about it the prop. that it didn't: it would simply have been absent from the universe. But the hypothesis "It doesn't exist" though certainly false, doesn't seem to be meaningless: we can understand, since it *does* exist, what would be meant by its absence, & can see that that is something which *might* have been the case. And hence, in affirming that it is *not* the case we are affirming something.

All this, I'm afraid, is very obscure: & I don't feel certain what the truth is about it.

But I can put what seems to me to be the point at issue in another way.

Consider a particular sense-impression like that of this white cross. Now, when I have ceased to see it, I can know it by description, as *the* white sense-datum looking like a cross I was seeing just now. I do in fact know that there's one & only one thing of wh. it's true both that it was a white sense-datum looking like a cross, & that I was seeing it just now. That is to say, if we write $\phi =$ is a white cross seen by me just now, I know $E\,!\,(\imath x)(\phi x)$ $= (\exists c): \phi c : x \neq c . \supset_x . \sim \phi x$. Now R. maintains that if I say: that white cross I saw just now existed, all I can mean by this is this & this only: that there is no meaning of "is real" or "exists", such that I might mean: $(\exists c) : \phi c : x \neq c . \supset_x . \sim \phi x : c$ was real. But if, at the time when I saw it, I could have meant anything by "This exists", there must be such a meaning. It will be a meaning such that if $E\,!\,(\imath x)(\phi x)$ is true, it must be true too. But it won't be the case that the whole meaning of "That impression was real" is exhausted by $E\,!\,(\imath x)(\phi x)$.

Now if there is such a sense in which we can say that a particular impression is real, we shall be able to mean by "Sense-impressions are real", not only "There *are* sense-impressions", but also "*Every* sense-impression is *real*": & by all the sense-impressions that there are, *not* merely all sense-impressions but *all* that are real.

And if we can do so in the case of sense-impressions, it is possible (though I don't say certain) that in the case of material things, too, by "Material things are real", we may mean not only "There are material things", but "Every material thing is real". If material things are known to us by description as *the* thing of which this is a sense-impression, we shall.

⟨So that "This desk is real" will be capable of meaning not only There is something *of* which this is a sense-impression, but also: There's something of which it's true that this is *of* it, that this is *not of* anything other than it, & also that it's "real".⟩

This, however, still doesn't give us a sense in which "Material things are unreal" is *consistent* with There are material things: for, in this sense, if there are any material things, *every* material thing is real.

I come on now then to senses of "real", such that "All material things are unreal" or "Some material things are unreal", *both* have a meaning & are consistent with "There are material things". And there are only 3 such meanings that I know of.

(a) is the meaning or pair of meanings with which R. uses the term "real", e.g. in the last of his lectures on the Philosophy of Logical Atomism (*Monist*, July 1919, pp. 364 foll.: everyone should read them: they occur in *Monist*, Oct. 1918 & 3 foll.).[1] His last lecture is called "What there is?" You'll find he there says (p. 365) "One purpose that has run through all that I have said, has been the justification of analysis, i.e., the justification of logical atomism, of the view that you can get down in theory, if not in practice, to ultimate simples, out of which the world is built, and that those simples have a kind of reality not belonging to anything else. Simples, as I tried to explain, are of an infinite number of sorts. There are particulars and qualities and relations of various orders, a whole hierarchy of different sorts of simples, but all of them if we were right, have in their various ways some kind of reality that doesn't belong to anything else". He goes on to say that there's no reason to think that this *desk* is such a simple: that it may be merely what he calls "a logical fiction"— as to what he means by this I shall presently have a lot to say. And then he goes on to say that in saying that desks are "logical fictions" he is maintaining "the unreality of things we think real". And he goes on to insist on what he calls the "reality of things we think unreal". He says phantoms & hallucinations "have the most complete & absolute & perfect reality that anything can have". And he goes on to say that "the things that are really real last a very short time" (p. 371). In this he is purely mistaken in supposing that phantoms & hallucinations, in the sense in which he supposes them to be "real", are by anyone supposed to be unreal. Nobody supposes that the drunkard's sense-impressions are unreal: it is only the snakes he sees which are unreal, & his impressions are not the snakes he sees.

Now what does he mean by "real" here?

I think we can detect 2 meanings: (1) = simple, or ultimate constituent of the world (p. 371)

(2) that particular kind of simple, which he calls a "particular", since it is only these, not qualities & relations, that can be said to "last only a very short time".

We get here a fairly clear meaning for "real" & "unreal": to say material objects are "unreal" may mean merely (a) that they're not simples, (b) not particulars; & of course the prop.

---
[1] [Reprinted in B. Russell, *Logic and Knowledge* (London, 1956).]

that they are not is perfectly consistent with "There are material things".

It seems to me perfectly possible, nay probable, that R. is right in saying that material things are not simples: & it seems to me very likely that it's not only R. who uses "real" in this sense, but that many use it = "particular". When people talk of "the real" they may mean this.

⟨I think people who say that the Absolute alone is real, probably mean (though they don't know they do) that it's the only particular.⟩

The only other meaning I can think of is one in which "real" = having value, = "good"—it's a term of approval. We do so use it in "is a real man". And that seems to me the only definite sense involved e.g. in Bradley's use of it. And of course it is a sense in wh. reality can have degrees.

This is of course perfectly consistent with "There are material things". It may well be the case that, though there are, yet none of them have any value; still less are perfect.

IV

DO WE KNOW THAT MATERIAL
THINGS ARE REAL?

Suppose we are presented with an argument designed to shew
either

(1) Nothing has shape or size, or Nothing is extended

(2) No proposition of the form "There *have been* extended
things" is true

(3) Whenever we judge "This is a material thing", we are
mistaken.

If I'm right, from each of these props. there will follow "Nature
is not real"; & each has been believed to be more likely true than
not by some philosophers.

Can we *refute* any of these props.? i.e. *prove* them to be untrue.
I think we can.

In order to refute a given prop. q, all that you need to do is to
find some prop. p, which (1) you *know* to be true, which (2) is
inconsistent with the prop. in question, & (3) is such that in arguing "Since p therefore not q" you are not arguing in a circle:
e.g. in order to refute "There are no black swans" you have only
to find a black swan, i.e. to find a prop. of the form "This is a
swan & is black", which you *know* to be true.

Now consider (1) I refute "Nothing has shape or size" by
pointing to the prop. "This desk has shape & size".

Isn't this a conclusive refutation?

I think it is.

People who say that it isn't will be apt to use 3 arguments

(a) They will say the argument is a *petitio principii* = *circulus
in probando*.

But this seems to me a mere mistake—the same mistake which
Keynes points out pp. 425 foll.[1]

It is perfectly true that "This desk has shape" is something
which can only be true if "Nothing has shape" is false, & you
may perhaps say, if you like, that "something has shape" is
contained in it. But I should be guilty of *petitio principii* only if

---

[1] [J. N. Keynes, *Formal Logic*, 4th ed. (London, 1906).]

44

my knowledge that this desk had shape was based on a prior knowledge that "Some things have shape": only if we could say, "I shouldn't have known this, if I hadn't first known the other". And obviously this isn't true, any more than the knowledge, on the part of the first person who saw a black swan, "This is a swan & is black" was based on a prior knowledge "There are black swans".

You are guilty of *petitio principii* in offering p as a proof of q, only if your knowledge that p, or that p is probable, was not *independent* of your knowledge that q or that q is probable, i.e. was based upon it. This is what Johnson (II. 10)[1] expresses badly by saying: your asserting of p *has implied* a previous asserting of q.

⟨*Circular proof*

It is natural to say:

If S (1) knows (p) "Whatever the bible says is true; & the bible says God exists", & (2) *sees* that from this there follows (q) "God exists", then S has proved that God exists.

But this is not the case.

S will not have proved that God exists, unless *the* knowledge of p from which he inferred q was *independent of* any knowledge of q: = unless he would have had *that* knowledge of p, even if he had not known q previously, nor known previously anything else from which q followed.

If his knowledge of p is dependent on his knowledge of (r) "The bible was inspired by God; & whatever is said in a book inspired by God is true" then it is dependent on a previous knowledge of something else from which q follows.⟩

(b) They may say: You don't *know* "This desk has shape".

This is an argument which I shall discuss under: Do we know that Nature is real?

(c) They may say: "This desk has shape" is false, because it is self-contradictory.

Now the argument: "This desk has shape" is true ∴ it is not self-contradictory

is just as good an argument as

"This desk has shape" is self-contradictory ∴ it is false.

⟨What I can't understand is how anybody can think their argument a better one.⟩

[1] [W. E. Johnson, *Logic*, Part II (Cambridge, 1922).]

We can argue: The premisses offered as shewing that "This desk has shape" is self-contradictory, either *cannot* be true or cannot shew it, bec. "This desk has shape" [is true].

People don't see this, I think: *If* you know that this desk has shape, then it follows that the argument used to shew that it is self-contradictory *must* be invalid—either the premisses are false, or they don't shew it. This really is a conclusive proof, *provided* you know that the desk has shape.

Exactly the same argument may be used in both the other 2 cases.

But there is an additional argument which can be used against (3) & not against (1) & (2).

(1) & (2) are not self-contradictory; but (3) is.

This arises from the fact that (3) is a prop. about *our judgments*: It asserts "*We* do make judgments of the form "This is a material thing" ". But what does *we* mean? It means "men with human bodies living on the earth"; & this means men related to material things related to *this* material thing.

I said there are other things to be said:
Denial that there are physical things involves certain consequences, not commonly seen.

(1) Philosophers who deny it, almost all, not only admit but insist that *we* do make such judgments as "This is a desk" & so on.

The prop. that *we* make such judgments entails there are physical things. For [it means] human beings who have had bodies, which lived upon the earth, have made such judgments, during the lifetime of their bodies.

A philosopher who denies physical things need not be a Solipsist; but he must deny the existence of any *men*, in ordinary sense, beside himself.

(2) Philosophers who deny it almost all make props. about the proper use of words.

This involves the "we".

(3) Philosophers who deny it refer to the opinions of other philosophers. They always mean by this human philosophers, who have had bodies & lived on the earth, & refer to opinions wh. they held during the lifetime of their bodies.

If human philosophers have denied the reality of physical things, then there certainly are physical things.

It follows that I can't consistently regard the fact that other human philosophers have held that there are no physical things as a reason which gives some probability that there are none. For *if* they have, then there are physical things. I can't work this out, I give it as a suggestion.

(4) They imply that *it's not true* that the earth existed more than 6000 years ago: i.e. that all scientific judgments are false.

Do we know that Nature is real? I distinguish this from the question: Is Nature real? both because the prop. "Nature is real" does not necessarily entail "We know it to be so"; bec. in fact a very large number of philosophers seem to me to have held the view that Nature is real, while at the same time holding that we don't *know* it to be so; & bec. although arguments to shew that Nature is not real will necess. shew also that we don't know it to be so, people who hold the view just mentioned use different arguments.

I should explain that by "know" I mean "know for certain"— wh. is tautological. And one thing is clear at once that "know" not = believe truly; for I certainly do either know or believe that Nature is real, & if Nature were real & know = believe truly, it would follow that I *know*. This is a point often not seen. But proved by Russell. (*Problems of Philosophy*, p. 205.)

What people commonly say is: We do all believe these; they are Beliefs of Common Sense; but they *may* be false = we don't know for certain that they aren't, in any particular case, though in fact they often aren't false.

And others say: They are matters of Faith—meaning not of Knowledge. Faith is perhaps sometimes used as opp. not to knowledge, but to reasoned knowledge; i.e. so that Faith can be merely a species of knowledge. It seems to me perfectly evident that if we're to have reasoned knowledge of anything, we must have unreasoned knowledge of some things. So that to say that such props. were matters of Faith, *not* of Reason, wouldn't necessarily exclude their being known. But commonly people are, I think, forgetting or denying this, & if they say these are mere matters of Faith, mean that they are not known.

What is meant is: "*It's certain that* we all do believe many such props., but none of us *know* any of them to be true".

And what's meant by "*It's certain that . . .*" is

"I & many other men *know* that we all do believe many such props., but none of us *know* any of them to be true".

This is self-contradictory, because if *I* know that other *men* have believed such props., I know that the earth has existed & that human bodies have existed; & hence if *we* all know these things we *know* this; & if we know that other human beings have existed, we certainly *know* a prop. of the form "There have been material things".

It seems to me philosophers overlook this point in the most amazing way. They hold it's quite certain that *men* believe these things, that they are beliefs of Common Sense; & yet that it's not certain that there are any men.

But "We *know* that men believe these things, but we don't know that any such props. are true" is self-contradictory.

My point is that when people say: "*We* believe such things" they commonly mean, "It's *certain* that we believe them"; & by this, not only, *I* know that we believe them: though even that would be self-contradictory, since *we* don't know, includes *I* don't know.

I can only appeal to you to ask whether that isn't really what you are meaning. A dogmatic form of statement usually implies "It is certain that". But this is a point about which I feel uncertain.

The same comes in merely if you say: "We don't know".

This means "it's *certain* that other men have existed, but none of them have known".

Nobody, in fact, means only: "*I* don't know, &, *if* other men have existed similar to me, they don't know either".

I ask you whether philos. who say things about "we" are actually only in the state wh. would be naturally expressed by "I believe that there have been other men beside myself, & that they have made judgments of this sort".

It seems to me quite plainly not: they certainly think they *know* it.

In all this, however, I am assuming that *I* know how other men use language! or, if not, what am I assuming?

There certainly is, however, no self-contradiction in the position: There have been other men, & they have made these judgments, but they haven't ever known any to be true.

There is only self-contrad. in holding *I know* there have been other men, & they have made these judgments, but they haven't known them to be true.

But in fact, I think, everybody who has held [the former] has held [the latter].

I can ask myself: Do *I* know that that is a physical thing?

And I *know* (I think) that other philosophers have given the following reasons why they think I'm unreasonable if I answer that I *do* know for certain.

Have they? do I know it? do I know it's probable? If I don't know that it's a blackboard, I don't know *any* of these things.

But what are the reasons?

(a) You don't know for certain, anything wh. you *can* doubt. And you *can* doubt that is a blackboard.

I really don't know whether I *can*. Nor do I know that if I *can*, that proves that I don't know it.

⟨People who say this seem to me confusing "indubitable" = not able to be doubted with "indubitable" = known. To doubt is to believe a prop. of the form "Perhaps this isn't a blackboard" & to believe that is to believe *you don't know it*. But mayn't you believe this, even when you do know it?⟩

(b) In hallucinations & dreams you feel certain that so-&-so is a lion or a house, & yet you are wrong. ∴ Judgments like this are sometimes wrong; i.e. this *may* be wrong.

I want to consider the bare question: Do *I* know of the existence of Nature? ⟨But, *if* I do, then certainly others do.⟩ Are there argum. wh. ought to convince me that I don't?

This is a view which may be held in 2 forms:

What are the reasons for saying we don't know?

Is there anything that ought to convince me personally that I don't know this is a blackboard?

(1) That sometimes, e.g. in dreams & hallucinations, we think we know a prop. of this form to be true, when in fact we don't.

⟨You will find this arg. given in Russell's *Outline*.[1] Therefore it's *possible* in any particular case that you are mistaken. Is it *possible* I am mistaken in "This is a blackboard"? *Not*, if I know it. What does the argument prove? There are experiences wh. resemble this in a certain respect & wh. are false beliefs, ∴ this one *may be* a false belief. I.e. *some* of its characters are compatible

---

[1] [B. Russell, *An Outline of Philosophy* (London, 1927).]

with its being a false belief. I don't see how this can give any good reason for thinking this is not a case of knowledge.⟩

If such a view says: We *know* that in some cases we are mistaken, it is self-inconsistent: for we can certainly only *know* that in a particular case "This exists" was *not* true, by inference from cases in wh. we know that it *is* true.

This is the form in wh. this argument is generally used.

But a person might say *he* or *we* only know that it's *highly probable* we are sometimes mistaken; & I can't see that he need then be guilty of a logical absurdity.

I *certainly* do at present either know or believe that this is a physical thing.

That is (*certainly* means this) I *know* that I either know or believe it.

But suppose I don't: how am I to argue the question with myself whether I know it or not?

One last argument that has been suggested to me is this.

(1) No human being has ever known immediately: This is a physical thing.

(2) No human being has ever known this by formal deduction exclusively from premisses that were known immediately.

(3) Part of the reasons for the conclusion: "This is a physical thing" has in every case been of an inductive nature: it is a conclusion based on past experience, i.e. facts immediately known by me in the past, none of which were of the nature "This is a physical thing", or entailed it.

(4) Reasons of an inductive nature never *prove* any stronger conclusion than: It's highly probable that p. That is, anything I *know*, in consequence of them, must always be of the form "It's highly probable that this is a physical thing": I can never *know* in this way "This *is* a physical thing".

From the premisses it would follow I don't *know* "This is a physical thing"; but that I not merely believe it, but do know "It is highly probable this is a physical thing".

Now I don't feel perfectly certain of (1) & (2): I shall discuss them presently: whether they are true partly depends on *what* I am believing or knowing when I believe or know "This is a physical thing", i.e. on the analysis of this prop. or fact.

But, if they're true, & (4) is true, the conclusion follows: & (4)

is something for which I believe there is very high authority; Johnson, Keynes & Broad are all agreed about it.

But why? Do I in fact know this? I can't understand *how* such a prop. as this can be known, except on the basis of a number of cases of immediate knowledge to the effect "It's only known that this is highly probable", "This was arrived at by induction".

⟨It's itself an induction: you examine all the cases of conclusions known by induction, & *find* that they're all only of the form "it's highly probable that p".⟩

And I don't dispute that in many cases I do know this. I think I don't know for certain that the sun will rise tomorrow—only that it's highly probable. But that this is *always* the case with conclusions arrived at by induction, I am not satisfied.

Broad (*Mind*, Oct. 1918)[1] is the only one who, so far as I know, has tried to prove it.

He says "I propose to try to prove 3 points".

(1) *Unless* inductive conclusions be expressed in terms of probability all inductive inference *involves a formal fallacy*.

And he goes on to say "I believe this first point can be rigorously established".

I will try to say what I think he means:

If you infer p from a set of inductive premisses, & p is *not* of the form "it is probable that q" you are *guilty of a formal fallacy*.

It is not a *valid form of inference* (p. 391) if you infer p from a set of inductive premisses, if p is not of the form "it is probable that q".

And this means more definitely: You cannot *know* p as a consequence of an inductive arg., unless p is of this form.

Now, regarded as an argument to establish the latter conclusion, it seems to me that his argument itself involves a formal fallacy.

It is of the general form that: an inductive arg. is from "All observed S's are P" to "All S's are P"; & that this is always a formal fallacy, whatever other premisses you take.

This, of course, does not apply directly to eduction: but "All past S's have been observed to be P", therefore this S is P (though this is not observed).

Now what does this prove? That the conclusion All S's are P, or This S is P, does not follow *formally* or *deductively* from the premisses.

Certainly it doesn't.

[1] [C. D. Broad, "On the Relation between Induction and Probability (I)".]

But it's a formal fallacy to infer that, because it doesn't follow deductively, it doesn't *follow*: i.e. that the argument doesn't *prove* it: that you don't *know* the conclusion.

If you *know* p in consequence of these premisses, you don't know it *deductively*.

But from the fact that it's not known formally, it doesn't follow that it's not known.

Broad in inferring [from] "p is not proved formally by the premisses q, r, s—& these are the only premisses you have", "p isn't proved at all".

This is a thing wh. *doesn't* itself follow formally: acc. to me it *may* nevertheless be a good argument. But if B. were right, it couldn't be.

What I ask is: Why shouldn't premisses wh. don't prove a conclusion formally yet *prove* it? Why shouldn't you *know* a thing in consequence of certain premisses, in spite of the fact that it doesn't follow formally from them?

Broad urges in favour of his conclusion that we never know, in consequence of inductive premisses, anything except "It's highly probable that", the difference between "All grass is green" & "2 + 2 = 4". He says we *always* admit that the opposite of an inductive conclusion is *possible*. So we do in this case. But suppose my present conclusion "I'm now seeing a blackboard" as opp. to "I'm having an hallucination of one" or "I'm dreaming of one" is an inductive conclusion. Do we admit it there? And is there any reason why we should?

All args. to *prove* that I *don't* know that this is a physical thing, seem to me obviously weak.

All must necessarily assume: "I *do* know this", & it seems to me much more doubtful whether I do know the thing in question, than whether I know this.

I can't prove that I *know* it; but I think I do.

And if *I* do, you do too: I agree with the philosophers who assume (quite against their principles) that it is *certain* that all human beings are in the same boat in this respect.

I don't of course say that *all* human beings know these things: *that* isn't meant by *we*.

But though some of you may *think* you don't know them, while I think I do: if *I* do, you certainly do know them, in spite of thinking you don't: just as, if you don't, I certainly don't either, in spite of thinking I do.

V

SENSE-DATA AND SENSE-QUALITIES

Some people both use & understand the term "sense-data" to mean the same as (1) the term "sense-qualities" or (2) absolutely specific sense-qualities or (3) sense-qualities which are given to somebody or (4) absolutely specific sense-qualities which are given to somebody.

I don't use "sense-data" in any of these ways—or at least I *think* I don't: for there are some people who maintain that the very things which I call sense-data are in fact sense-qualities: in which case my usage would be (4), though I think it isn't.

It seems to me very important to distinguish the things which I call sense-data from sense-qualities. The things which I call sense-data are in my view certainly "particulars", not qualities at all; so that the 2 classes "sense-data" & "sense-qualities" are mutually exclusive; nothing which belongs to the one belongs to the other. And, of course, there is nothing in the name sense-data to shew this: some sense-qualities are undoubtedly in a sense "given" & given by sense. The 2 classes are, it seems to me, very frequently confused.

Sense-qualities appear to be what Whitehead means by sense-objects—& of course by this name he suggests that they are the only things which can properly be said to be sense-*data*.

Sense-qualities themselves may be divided into 2 classes: those which are absolutely specific, & those which are generic: or, in Johnson's language, those which are absolutely determinate = not sub-determinate to any other quality, & those which are more or less indeterminate = are sub-determinate each to several other qualities. The distinction between these 2 classes seems to me of the utmost importance, & often overlooked. "Blue", "red" & "yellow" are generic sense-qualities—at least when we mean by them qualities which sensibly appear to belong to sense-data: "blue", "red" & "yellow", in the sense in which physical objects have these colours, are, of course, very likely not sense-qualities at all: this is again a distinction which is very frequently overlooked; people very often suppose that if this piece of chalk is white at all, it must have the sense-given quality "white": they

53

think that what we mean by saying that it is white, is that it has the sense-given quality; & concluding for various more or less good reasons that it hasn't got that, they think themselves bound to deny that it is white at all. In my view, it's perfectly certain that the assertion "it is white", in the sense we mean it, is true, but highly doubtful whether it has the sense-given quality: from which it follows that it's highly doubtful whether "white" in the sense in which it does belong to physical objects is the sense-given quality.

Assuming that you understand what I mean by sense-given qualities, or sense-qualities, the distinction between those which are absolutely specific & those which are generic is plain enough. "Blue" is generic because it is sub-determinate both to "Cambridge blue" & to "Oxford blue"; "red" is generic because it is sub-determinate both to "scarlet" & to "crimson". But "Cambridge blue" & "scarlet" are also generic: there are many slightly different shades all of which are shades of Cambridge blue, & so of scarlet. In fact absolutely every colour which can be *named* is generic: & I think the same is true of absolutely every sense-quality which can be named. You might think there is an exception to this in such qualities as "exactly circular" or "exactly square": "circular" & "square" themselves are clearly generic. But it seems to me that even "exactly circular" is so too: for a sense-datum can't sensibly appear to be so, without also appearing to be of a particular size, & it seems to me that "exactly circular & of this size", though it appears to be a conjunctive property, is not really so, but is super-determinate to "exactly circular", just as "scarlet" is to "red". Similarly you might think that the quality of being of the pitch of the A of a tuning-fork at concert pitch is absolutely determinate: but no auditory sense-datum can sensibly appear to be of that pitch without being of some special timbre or quality; & to be of this special quality & that pitch, is, it seems to me, super-determinate to being of that pitch. And we have no names for these special timbres: even different tuning-forks will be of slightly different ones. I think therefore it is true that absolutely specific sense-qualities never have any names: that any sense-quality which has a name is generic.

Now, whenever a sense-datum sensibly appears to have a generic quality, it always also sensibly appears to have an absolutely specific one. A sense-datum can't sensibly appear to be

Cambridge blue, without sensibly appearing to be of a particular nameless absolutely specific shade of Cambridge blue. And I think myself that "sensibly appearing to be Cambridge blue" is to be defined in terms of "sensibly appearing to be of an absolutely specific shade." To say "O *sensibly appears* to S to be Cambridge blue" = "O *sensibly appears* to S to have *some* shade which is a shade of Cambridge blue", where the second "sensibly appears" can't mean the same as the first. And similarly I think all *generic* qualities are *general* qualities: i.e. "O is Cambridge blue" = "O has *some* shade which is a shade of Cambridge blue", i.e. there is a quality of a quality (being a shade of Cambridge blue) such that "O is Cambridge blue" = "O has *some* quality of this quality". Similarly there is a quality, χ, of certain absolutely specific qualities, such that "O is red" = "O has *some* quality having χ". I.e. "being red" is to be defined in terms of "being a shade of red": it *looks* as if this were a circular def., but only bec. we have no simple name for the quality "being a shade of red".

But now, I said some people seem to suppose that the very things which I call sense-data are in fact sense-qualities. There is no question of their being *generic* sense-qualities, though I don't think people ever see this. If they are sense-qualities at all, they must be absolutely specific ones. Can they be? Is it possible that what I mean by "sense-data" is "absolutely specific sense-qualities that are given to some one"? Are corresponding objects[1] qualities?

The American people who call themselves Critical Realists seem to hold this: they hold that *nothing* is "given" but essences; & seem to mean by "essences" absolutely specific sense-qualities, or patterns of such.

How is one to argue the view that corresponding objects are not qualities at all, but particulars?

It seems to me that the contrary view is a sheer mistake; but I don't know how to argue it.

The difference can be put in this way. *Given* sense-qualities are entities which sensibly appear to some-one to belong to something. Sense-data are entities to which sense-qualities sensibly appear to some-one to belong. "Sensibly appears" is a triadic relation, & not a symmetrical one.

But how is this to be proved? You may have 2 different sense-

---

[1] [I.e. sense-data "corresponding" to material things. Cf. the next footnote.]

E

data which sensibly appear to have the *same* absolutely specific sense-qualities: every *internal* sensible quality which either appears to have the other [does] also. And since they are different, neither can be identical with any one, or the property of combining them. But then there are people who say that absolutely specific sense-qualities are *particular*: that no 2 sense-data ever have or sensibly appear to have the same: that what we *call* this is really having 2 different sense-qualities, exactly like one another.

This view seems to me to be in the last degree fantastic & one for which there is nothing whatever to be said: yet it is taken by Cook Wilson, Stout, Joseph, Kemp Smith: & I don't know how to refute it. Consider any considerable part of this blackboard which seems to you to be of a uniform black all over. The view implies that every part of that sense-datum sensibly appears to have a *different* sense-quality, though that which each sensibly appears to have is exactly like that which every other does. Thus the sensible absolutely specific shade of black which this whole appears to have is different, though exactly like, that which each of them appears to have! Could anything be more absurd! There could be no more flagrant instance of a multiplication of entities beyond necessity. The refutation perhaps is that: when I say "This sensibly appears to me to be of that shade" & "That sensibly appears to me to be of that shade", I am saying the *same* thing of this & that.

Suppose this colour is not identical with but only exactly like that, this shape & this size the same: why shouldn't we say that this *sense-datum* is merely the quality of uniting the 3 in a particular way?

If this sense-datum really does possess them all, they are undoubtedly united in a special way: the way in which they would be united if they all characterised anything else whatever: the way wh. we may express by saying that they all characterise *some* the same thing (though shape & size certainly characterise in a different sense from colour).

Why shouldn't we say that this sense-datum *doesn't* possess them all, but is identical with the property which anything which did would possess?

This, I think is what Santayana means by an essence.

I can see no objection to this, except (1) that when two sense-data look to you exactly alike in colour, the colour wh. the one sensibly appears to you to have is certainly *not* always different from that which the other does, nor the shape nor the size, & yet the sense-datum is: (2) that this couldn't "belong to" or characterise anything in the sense in which when 2 things are exactly alike in any internal respect they are characterised by the same quality.

One form in which this view that sense-data are qualities is apt to be implied is that of calling visual sense-data "colours". Nothing is a "colour" except a quality. Sense-data, on my view, are not "colours" but "coloured things". Yet you find people constantly talking of "colours" & "sounds" as if they were on a level. In the case of "sounds" we have no name corresponding to "colour"—a name which is the name of the *kind* of quality wh. belongs to sounds.

VI

SENSE-DATA, EVENTS AND CHANGE

I'm now going to take [an argument] wh. seems to me quite
independent of the assumption that s. d. have the properties they
sensibly appear to have, & wh. raises one or more tremendously
fundamental questions.

I look at this surface; then shut my eyes; then look at it again.
I can truly say: I *saw* this surface in the past.

But, people say: Of this sense-datum I can't truly say that I
saw it in the past: the corresponding s. d.[1] I saw in the past
may have been exactly like it, but was certainly *other* (existentially
other) than it.

∴ this sense-datum was *not* seen by me in the past; this surface
was; therefore this s. d. is not identical with this surface.

The first premiss seems to me quite certain: it's constantly
presupposed by things we know in common life; I can recognise
the *same* physical objects, & therefore also their surfaces.

The question is: Is it true that I didn't see this s. d. in the past?

Hume, & others, have assumed confidently that it is true; but
I can't see that it is self-evident. What arguments can be used?

(a) This sense-datum can't be identical with the one I saw
before, because it didn't exist in the interval during wh. my eyes
were shut.

⟨This is one of the things which distinguishes concrete things
from universals. This would give a reason for saying that no
particular can exist both now & in the past.⟩

This assumes that no *concrete* thing can exist at one time, go
out of existence, & then exist again; & I don't want to dispute
this, though I do want to call attention to it: I think very likely
it is a matter of def.

But I see no reason why it shouldn't have existed while my
eyes were shut: even if it were true, as Berkeley seems to hold,
that it can only exist when perceived, it won't follow that it didn't
exist, bec. all I know is that *I* didn't perceive it.

[1] [For the notion of a "corresponding sense-datum" see G. E. Moore, "The
Nature of Sensible Appearances", *Aristotelian Soc., Supplementary Vol. VI*
(1926).]

I think I can conceive clearly that it should have existed all the time, whether it has all the qualities it seems to have or not; *if* it does now while I look at it.

(b) That even when I keep looking at the object, I am continually seeing *new* sense-data, though the same surface: that in fact, no sense-datum wh. I see at any time has ever been seen by me in the past.

This seems to me to be a contention of the same order as the contention that all sense-data really have the qualities they appear to have, though quite independent of it: i.e. it may, I think, *really* be self-evident, though I can't see that it is so: & the question whether it is so or not seems to me to be a very fundamental question, like that one. I.e. it's a question on which hosts of other philosophical questions depend. It's also a question as to wh. it seems to me extremely difficult to be sure.

It seems to me it *would* be self-evident, if it were self-evident that every sense-datum is an *event*. I don't think it's identical with this: I suppose even if sense-data were not events, it *might* be true; but I don't see how it could then possibly be self-evident. But it may, I think, be self-evident that sense-data are events; & if so it would follow that no present s. d. can possibly have existed in the past. It is one of the *marks* of an event that no present event can possibly have existed before.

Whitehead, Johnson & Broad (& now R.) all seem to assume that sense-data are *events* (Whitehead, of course, holds that *sense-objects* aren't: but what I call sense-data he seems to hold are—& not only so but physical events); but so far as I can see without discussion.

And with regard to sense-data, Broad expresses the assumption in question (apart from the question whether they're events) in the following way:

Talking of the assumption with regard to 2 successive sensible fields, [he says] that "a sensum in one field is *ipso facto* different from any sensum in another field".[1] He says this is partly a matter of def.; by wh. he means that if you used "sensum" in the same way as he proposes to use "sense-object", it would not be true. To say this is to say that his def. of sensum was not unambiguous, since it ought to have made clear that a sensum was not a sense-object.

[1] [C. D. Broad, *Scientific Thought* (London, 1923), p. 346.]

What, acc. to him, is *not* a matter of def.? That, if you're *not* using sensum = sense-object, then in a case where you have 2 successive perceptions that don't overlap, every sensum in the field perceived in the earlier perception is *past* at the time at which you have the later perception, & every sensum in the field perceived in the later is present at the time when you have that later perception.

⟨Successive sense-fields = *not* sense-fields such that one is wholly *past* relatively to the other, but such that the presentation of one to me is wholly past relatively to that of the other.⟩

He then says it is *obvious* that what is now past can't be precisely & numerically identical with what is now present.

But what is *not* obvious to me is that every sensum perceived at the earlier time *is past* at the time at wh. I have the later perception.

All that *is* obvious is that it *existed in the past*, & it's by no means obvious that what existed in the past can't be precisely & numerically identical with what exists now.

If you mean by a *past* sensum, one wh. you saw at a past time, then it isn't obvious to me that it can't be precisely & numerically identical with what I see now.

I want to make as clear as possible what the issue is: bec. it seems to me a very fundamental one, of distinguishing notions wh. language easily leads us to confuse.

A existed in the past is not inconsistent with *A exists now*.

But there is a sense of "past" such that "A is past" is inconsistent with "A is present": namely that which applies to events.

The whole question is: Do I know with regard to the corresponding s. d. I saw before I closed my eyes that it is *past*, or merely that it *existed in the past*?

I don't see how I *could* know the former, unless I know that every s. d. is an event: in that case, I *could* know it, since every event wh. I saw before now *must* be past now (though things wh. are not events may be past too). I cannot see that visual & tactual sense-data *are* events: that as I watch this piece of chalk, this sense-datum may not be precisely identical with what I saw just now.

As for the premiss that I *did* see this surface in the past, that seems to me perfectly certain. We can *recognise* physical objects;

& they may be the same even if we don't recognise them. *Events* we never can recognise.

People who deny that we see the same surface are really doing so bec. they think the sense in wh. this surface I see now is the *same* as that I saw just now, is not the same as that in which the white cross enclosed with this ring is the same as the white cross that is on the blackboard. Probably, I think, almost certainly, the sense is not the same, but of course that isn't *the* sense in wh. we commonly use the words.

This argument, therefore, as it stands, seems to me inconclusive bec. I can't feel sure that it's ever true that I haven't seen the same corr. s. d. in the past.

An argument liable to be confused with the last; but which I'm inclined to think is really conclusive.

Often true:

"This surface may have been internally different a minute ago"

"This sense-datum can't have been internally different a minute ago".

By "internally different" I mean having different internal or intrinsic properties: & by "internal properties" I mean such properties as (1) qualities, like size, shape & colour; (2) the having or not having a particular part, say A, so that if, for instance, a microscopic particle of chalk dust has fallen off this chalk line, since a minute ago, this chalk line will be internally different from what it was then, simply because that particular particle was then a part of it, & is not now; (3) any property which consists in having its parts arranged in a particular way relatively to one another: e.g. even supposing the same individual electrons are contained in this chalk line as were a minute ago, yet if they changed their relative positions since then, the line will be internally different, simply because it had then the property "these parts of it are arranged in *this* pattern" & has now the property "these parts of it are arranged in *this* different pattern".

And by "may have been" I mean merely that the proposition that it is so is not self-contradictory; by "can't have been" that it is.

⟨To say "A is exactly like B" = A has no internal property which B hasn't, nor B which A. Nobody uses exactly like to include properties consisting in relation to external things (= *not* parts) e.g. nobody, except a philosopher, would say that the fact that this & that are differently related to this line, prevented this from being exactly like that.⟩

This argument, provided the premisses are true in any particular case, will be absolutely conclusive that *in that case* the surface & the sense-datum are not identical, since of the one something is true which is not true of the other: & then, in virtue of our general principle, if it is true in any case that a corr. s. d. is not identical with the surface it represents, it will be so in all.

And it raises an issue of fundamental philosophical importance —comparable to that raised by the last, namely whether all sense-data are events—namely the problem of *internal change*: what is meant by saying that a thing changes *internally*. People often talk of "*the* problem of change" as if it were only one. But it seems to me there are several; & that in particular the problem of internal change is quite a different one from that of change in respect of external relations to other things. There is obviously a broad difference between the two which everyone sees. My body is constantly changing its position relatively to the sun & the stars, owing both to the revolution of the earth on its axis, & to its movement round the sun. But it wouldn't follow from that that it's changing internally, except on the views of those who say that no relations are purely external—a consequence of which is that nothing can change its relations to other external things (= not parts of it) without changing internally. But even those who take this view are bound to admit that there is a difference between the meaning of *internal* change & *external* change, since they can only define their view by saying that a difference of relational properties always involves a difference of internal properties. And internal change does obviously exist: my body changes internally (in way 3) every time my heart beats. External change, in itself, raises no problems but the general problems of time. But internal change raises a quite different & independent problem, which seems to me to be of extreme difficulty & not to have been satisfactorily treated by anybody.

By internal change I mean a sort of change which can only happen to a *continuant*: which happens when & only when the *same* continuant exists at two different times, & has at the one an internal property which it has not got at the other. It's necessary to say this, because there is a certain sense in which events also can change internally: namely when one temporal part of an event has a different internal property which a later part of the same has not got. Every temporal part of an event is also an event; & very often one of these contained events has internal properties which another has not got. E.g. the whole event which consists in my grasping this book; or a note which begins soft & gradually gets louder. In general an event which changes internally is what is meant by a *process*; & people often use "process" = "event". But I think this is entirely a mistake. There's no reason why there shouldn't be events which involve *no* change at all: such that every event which is a part of them is *exactly alike* in internal properties to every other. But the point I am at present concerned with is that the sense in wh. an event changes internally is quite different from that in which a continuant does. About the former there's no special problem, except the general problems of time. But about the latter there *is* a very special problem. Of course, there would not be if Broad were right in saying that "a thing is simply a long event, of a particular kind" (*Sc. Th.*, p. 393). But in saying so it seems to me he is quite certainly wrong. He only says so because he has confused two quite distinct props. with one another, as I am going to try to explain.

Having said all this, we can express the above argument as follows

(1) This surface is a *mutable* continuant = the *sort* of continuant which it is not self-contradictory to suppose to change internally

(2) This sense-datum is *not* a mutable continuant.

And this is a way of bringing out the difference between this & the last argument which was

(1) This surface is a continuant (= may have existed in the past)

(2) This sense-datum *cannot* have existed in the past. ⟨For an event can only exist in the past by being past, & a present event *can't* be past.⟩

I'm by no means certain that sense-data are not *continuants* —that's why I thought the last argument inconclusive. But it does seem to me practically certain that they're not *mutable* continuants—that's what I'm going now to argue: & hence, even if it did then exist, can't be identical with the surface. And why the 2 arguments are liable to be confused, is because people in general do not distinguish between being a *mutable* continuant, & being a continuant. They think (perhaps rightly) that whatever is a continuant must be a *mutable* continuant. I don't think this is certain; &, even if it is so, it needs to be expressly argued.

Now let's consider the argument

(1) This surface *is* a mutable continuant. You don't know that there wasn't a particle of chalk which formed part of it a minute ago & which doesn't now: there *may* be, in that sense: & hence also it's *not* self-contradictory.

We've got to stick to this that there are things which exist at 2 different times, & yet have different internal properties at the 2 times. Consider the West Front of King's Chapel. We've all of us seen it several times: and it has existed for more than 300 years. Yet some of the stones of which it is built have been replaced by others—perhaps they all have by now; the stones have weathered & so on.

We can *recognise* the same object: we've seen it before. My face is the *same* face you saw on Tuesday, & you know it's the same. And yet it has almost certainly changed internally. The only question is, in what sense it's the *same*; & this seems to me a really difficult question. Recognising *things* is quite different from recognising qualities.

(2) This sense-datum *can't* have had different internal properties a minute ago, even if it existed a minute ago.

Why not?

I think this is something which it's extremely difficult to explain; & I may be wrong about it; but I feel there is a real difficulty.

Let's try to put it first in this way. I feel that if A has an internal property Q at t_1, & B has not got Q at t_2, A *must* be other than B: that it can't be A which has not got Q at t_2. This is exactly the same sort of thing which people say to prove that no relational properties are purely external. But about *them* I feel no difficulty at all. It seems to me perfectly easy to conceive how exactly the same thing should be at one time only an inch from the blackboard, at another a yard. But with *internal* properties it does seem to me difficult.

But now, it won't do to put the argument in this form; because now we're denying (1). What I really wanted to say & to make you see is only that there's *one* sense of "*same*" in which a thing which has the internal property Q at t_1 can't be the same as a thing which hasn't got Q at t_2. We have to stick to it that there is a sense in which it can.

But how are you to point out & make clear to yourself *what* the sense is?

There is *a* sense of "x had q at t_1" such that this is a *conjunctive* prop. = "x existed at t_1 *and* had q"; a sense, that is to say, such that having an intrinsic property at a time does not involve an *ultimate* triadic relation between the thing, the property & the time, but involves the notion of a thing having a property *timelessly*, i.e. a meaning of x *has* q, such that this does *not* mean has *now* q, or *had* at some time q.

Now, with this meaning of "having a property" it's impossible that a given thing should both have & not have the same property: it's impossible that anything should both timelessly have q, & also timelessly not have q.

Consequently with *this* meaning of "having q at t_1" & "not having q at t_2" it's impossible that anything whatever should have q at t_1 & not have q at t_2.

Since what this means is

a existed at t_1 & has *timelessly* q

a exists at t_2 & has *timelessly* not q

& though it's perfectly possible that a should have existed at both, it's not possible that anything should *timelessly* have a certain property & also timelessly not have it.

I insist on this point, because it's often, & rightly, said that the fact that having q at t_1 is incompatible with not having q at t_1 (which is always the case), does not entail that having q at t_1 is incompatible with not having q at t_2. In *general* this is true; but in particular cases having q at t_1 *is* incompatible with not having q at t_2. It all depends on the analysis of "has q at t_1". Where this = "exists at t_1, & has timelessly q", "had q at t_1" *is* incompatible with "has not q at t_2". It does not *always* mean this: e.g. "Queen Anne's death was at one time *not* past" is not incompatible with "Queen Anne's death was at one time past". From which it follows that "Queen Anne's death is now past" is *not* analysable into "Queen Anne's death exists now, & is timelessly past"— which is obvious enough, as regards the first part of it. When it is said that q is incompatible with not-q, it may be meant merely that having q at t_1 is incompatible with not having q at t_1; & the point to make is that *sometimes* this involves that having q at some time is incompatible with not having q at some time, & sometimes it isn't.

⟨Broad, *Sci. Thought*, p. 63.

Two things that puzzle me.

"On these grounds the whole long event is treated as the history of a single thing T".

He cannot mean that *every* long event which satisfies these conditions is so treated.

He must mean: Suppose anybody knows of the long event in question, *he* treats it as the history . . .

But what's meant by saying that: he "treats it as the history of. . ."

There are 2 different alternatives, which the use of this language conceals: as constantly happens in philosophy.

(1) It may mean: he will *say* or *think* "There is *some* thing, one & only one, such that this event is the history of it".

Or (2) There is *some* thing, one & only one, with regard to which he will *say* or *think* "This event is the history of *this* thing".

These 2 are constantly confused:

S is thinking that something is green

may mean

(1) There is something with regard to wh. S is thinking "This is green".

(2) S is thinking "Something is green".

The latter alternative is the only one consistent with what follows: he is contemplating our saying "*This thing* has changed from red to green".

But *how*, when we say this, are we using the expression "This thing"?

I think what B. is originally thinking is:

He will *say* "There is some thing, one & only one, of which this event is the history" meaning by these words *merely* "This event satisfies these conditions".

But merely to say this gives no answer at all to the question what is meant by "This event is the history of *this* thing".⟩

VII
PERCEPTUAL CONTINUITY

When you see the sun, your corr. s. d. exists at the time at which you're seeing it, but the phase of the sun's surface wh. you're seeing does *not* exist then, but existed about 8 mins. earlier. If so, the 2 must be different.

This is an argument which differs from all that I've hitherto considered, bec. it depends on premisses which are supposed to have been scientifically established. And I'm bound to say it seems to me a very strong one. But it doesn't in fact seem to me absolutely conclusive, as it does to many people: perhaps it ought to, but I confess I am in fact in doubt.

(1) Let's take here first the prop. that, suppose you are seeing the sun's surface at T, the phase of its surface which you are seeing does *not* exist at T, but existed about 8 mins. earlier than T.

It's easy to state 2 of the premisses on which this conclusion rests, but not by any means easy to see what the other premisses are which it requires.

The 2 are

(a) that the sun is about 90,000,000 miles distant from us

(b) that light travels at a velocity of about 300,000 km. a second.

These are both considered to be very well-established scientific props. but of very different orders: and I for one don't really doubt them a bit. But ought I to? According to many philosophers, & some scientific men themselves, they can't really be quite certain: they can only have a very high probability. And if I consider what reason *I* personally have for believing them, it rests entirely on my belief that there is a consensus of experts with regard to them: and this rests on my knowledge that other people on the earth have thought & done certain kinds of things: so that their certainty can't be greater, if as great, as my knowledge that this desk & blackboard are here now & at certain distances from one another. Moreover it's quite certain, I think, that how scientific men have arrived at it is from premisses of just this sort: knowledge about their instruments etc. And it may be said, when I see the sun I know with certainty that it exists now, just as I do that this desk does. It seems to me philosophers

67

are often guilty of inconsistency in supposing such scientific props. as these known to be true, while denying that we ever know such facts as that this is a desk—on which they rest. I can be much more certain that Einstein has existed & has held certain theories, than I can be that his theories are true.

But now, assuming that these 2 props. are certainly or almost certainly true, how does it follow that, if I see the sun at T, the phase of it I am then seeing does *not* exist at T, but only existed about 8 mins. before T?

Obviously there is required some such extra premiss as this: that, when I see a thing, the phase of it which I see is that which emitted those particular light-rays which caused my seeing of it.

This, I think, is usually taken for granted, & I don't doubt it; but I'm puzzled to know how it is known.

By the way, this argument is one, which, even to state it, requires the assumption that continuants have phases. I say, & rightly, that it's the surface of the sun I see. But this is a continuant. And the argument does not maintain that *it* doesn't exist when I see it. It is willing to allow that *it* may quite well. It only maintains that the "slice of its history" which I see is one wh. existed 8 mins. ago; or as R. puts it that what I see is "the sun of 8 mins. ago". But there's no such thing as "the sun of 8 mins. ago"; nor is it a slice of its history that I see: It's *it*, the surface of the sun: and it seems to me the only proper way to state it is to assume that a continuant is a logical constr. out of phases.

On this view, we should have to say that such statements as "The sun is shining now", or "There's a cloud between me & the sun", are either things which we don't know to be true, or what we mean by them is something different from what we mean by "This piece of paper is now between this blackboard & this desk". It seems to me we certainly are expressing something which we do know to be true; but are we *also* expressing something which we don't? Is what we say something which may be partially false? I raise this point because so many people hold that what we express by "This piece of paper is between me & this desk"—all common sense judgments—are *partially* false: I don't see how they can be; but it does seem to me there's some reason for saying so in this particular case.

(2) Is it certain that my sense-datum exists at T?

Many people hold that it is: that this is self-evident. And I think there's a great deal to be said for that view.

If our sense-data really have the qualities they appear to have, then I think it must be so; because then the existence of my sense-datum of the sun will be causally dependent on something wh. happened in my body less than 8 mins. ago; & hence the sense-datum can't be identical with something which used to exist 8 mins. ago.

This is a subject of which I know no satisfactory treatment anywhere; & it seems to me very complex & perplexing.

I'm going to introduce this by a quotation from Russell's *ABC of Atoms*[1]—the opening words.

"To the eye or to the touch, ordinary matter appears to be continuous; our dinner-table, or the chairs on which we sit, seem to present unbroken surface. We think that if there were too many holes the chairs would not be safe to sit on. Science, however, compels us to accept a quite different conception of what we are pleased to call 'solid' matter; it is, in fact, something much more like the Irishman's definition of a net, 'a number of holes tied together with pieces of string'. Only it would be necessary to imagine the strings cut away until only the knots were left."

R. says Science compels us to accept certain views as to physical surfaces like this of the blackboard.

And he says first that it compels us to accept the view that this surface *is* a number of different surfaces with empty space between them.

And what follows, taken with this, implies, though it does not *say*, that the surfaces in question are surfaces of electrons.

What it does say is that these surfaces are in the area wh. seems to us to be occupied by the surface of the blackboard; & that the greater part of this area is not really occupied at all.

He doesn't directly say the surface *is* the surface of these electrons.

This gives us one of our premises

viz. (1) a physical surface wh. we see very often *is* a number of different surfaces each separated from all the rest by empty intervals.

Now as to the other.

[1] [B. Russell, *The ABC of Atoms* (London, 1923).]

He says this surface *seems* to be continuous or unbroken—wh. is certainly true.

And the *"seems"* of course implies that the corr. s. d. either *sensibly appears* to be "continuous" or *is* so.

The corr. s. d. *is* continuous: entails: is not a number of discontinuous surfaces.

Let's take this argument.

Is the corr. s. d. continuous?

Why shouldn't we answer this by saying merely it sensibly appears to be so?

It seems to me we *can't* do this.

⟨For here to say that *it only sensibly appears* implies something positive about its internal properties. If a set of discontinuous things are to appear to be a continuous whole, this is not like a thing appearing to be yellow or elliptical; there must *be* a continuous whole, which the things in question appear to be identical with. There's a question raised of *what* it is that appears to be so-&-so: & I think it's imposs. that any discontinuous set of things, with which we're *acquainted*, should appear to be a continuous whole.⟩

I've suggested that a sense-datum may sensibly appear to be white, without anything whatever really being white; but it seems to me this is a different case: I want to suggest that it's impossible that a set of things should sensibly appear to form a continuous whole, unless something really is a continuous whole.

But this is a question which partly depends on what's meant by "forming a continuous whole". What are the fundamental notions involved?

This white line & that certainly are discontinuous = separated by an interval either of time or space.

But this white line *seems* to be a continuous whole: R. suggests perhaps it isn't: it *may* be suggested: *Nothing* is a continuous whole.

What's meant by saying that a set of things do form a continuous whole?

I think the answer depends on the analysis of a certain relation to which Whitehead has called attention, & which he calls that of "adjoining". He has suggested a certain analysis of it, which I think is correct; & if it is correct, then, I think, it's impossible that there should *seem* to be continuous wholes, unless there *are* continuous wholes.

The surface of that blackboard, as R. says, "appears to be continuous": it certainly does; there's no doubt about it: it appears to be a continuous whole.

But this means that the corr. s. d. *either* really is *or* sensibly appears to be continuous, in some sense or other. In *what* sense? We're asking *what* that property is which a corr. s. d. must possess or sensibly appear to possess, if the surface it represents is to be said to appear continuous: which is such that to say that the surface so appears is to say that the corr. s. d. wh. represents it *either* has that property *or* sensibly appears to have it.

And we're then going on to ask whether a sense-datum can sensibly appear to have it, without really having it.

And I want, first of all, to say something about what R. has to say about the meaning of the word "continuity" or "continuous".

This, as you all know, is a topic with which he has dealt again & again.

Take, e.g., Lecture V in *E.W.*[1] on the "theory of continuity", p. 131. He there tells us that "continuity, in mathematics, is a property only possible to a *series* of terms".

That is to say, the sense in wh. mathematicians use the word is one in which *series*, & nothing but series, can be continuous.

He says (132) that "math. have distinguished various degrees of continuity": which really means that they have used it in several *different* senses: but all the senses are senses in wh. nothing but a *series* can be continuous.

He says, for philosophical purposes, all that is important is the lowest degree called "compactness". I.e. that sense of "continuous" where "continuous" = "compact": no series is "continuous" in any of the other senses unless it is compact.

And this is a perfectly clear & easy notion: a series is compact if & only if between any 2 terms of it there is another. He points out that this is true of the series of fractions in order of magnitude.

E.g. $\frac{1}{2}$ & $\frac{51}{100}$; there's another greater than $\frac{1}{2}$ & less than $\frac{51}{100}$,

e.g. $\frac{101}{200}$; & whichever you take there will always be another.

This sense of "continuous" seems to me to be a perfectly clear one: the only thing that seems to me at all obscure about it

[1] [B. Russell, *Our Knowledge of the External World* (London, 1914).]

F

is what a "series" is. It's only series which can be continuous:
but what is a series? This is a question about wh. I wish he had
said more.

A series, he tells us, is "a set of terms arranged in an order".
⟨Might mean "Any set of terms of wh. it's true that they are
arranged in an order is a series", but that would not be true.⟩
"Numbers in order of magnitude" *are* a series. But the *set of
terms* itself isn't the series: it's only "a set of terms *in a certain
order*" which are a series. The same set of terms can be arranged
in different orders; & a given set, in one order, may be a compact
series, & in another *not* a compact series.

But what sort of an entity is "This set of terms in this order",
"The integers in order of magnitude"?

In *Introd.*, p. 34[1], he says baldly "A series is the same thing as
a serial relation".

And about the def. of a serial relation, there is no difficulty at
all: to say a relation is serial is to say that it is asymm., transitive,
& connected.

But obviously what we commonly mean by a series is *not* a
serial relation: it is certain terms *in* a certain serial relation. R.
practically admits this later when he says: "the ordinary relation
may be taken to *be* the series". And in the corresponding passage
in *Principia*, Vol. II, this is quite explicit: p. 498, "For our purposes, there is no use in distinguishing a series from its generating
relation . . . The generating relation completely determines the
series, and may, for all mathematical purposes, be taken to *be*
the series".

This is to admit that, after all, a serial relation *isn't* a series,
but only *determines* one. And I wish he had thought it worth
while to give a clear explanation of what a series is. It isn't true
that any set of terms, which actually are the field of a serial
relation, is a series. For the same set may be the field of 2 different
serial relations, P & Q; & the terms in question, *as related by P*,
will be one series; the same terms, *as related by Q*, another. The
terms themselves aren't a series at all. It's only "those terms *as
related by P*" which can be said to *be* a series, or to form a series.
And I'm sorry to say I can't explain what this means.

But now, starting from "continuity" = "compactness", R.
seems to wish to say that all philosophically important senses of

[1] [B. Russell, *Introduction to Mathematical Philosophy* (London, 1919).]

"continuity" can be defined in terms of "compactness": he never distinguishes any other sense; & he tries to argue that, in some sense or other, "mathematical continuity is adequate to the facts of sense".

Does he then really mean that the sense in which that sense-datum sensibly appears to be continuous, is that it sensibly appears to *be* a compact series, or that it sensibly appears to have a number of parts which form a compact series?

He never says so: & it seems to me perfectly certain that that can't be what we mean. It seems to me he never faces the question of what's meant by saying that a sense-datum "appears continuous", & that consequently there's a good deal of confusion in what he says.

In *E.W.* what he is chiefly concerned with is the question what's meant by saying that a given movement *is* continuous. He gives what he calls "the mathematical theory of continuous motion", which is defined in terms of compact series. And seems to wish to maintain, p. 141, that this theory will apply to the sense-datum we see when we actually see a motion: that there is actually a compact series of momentary views. Thus, p. 143, he distinguishes the questions

(1) Are compact series logically possible? (2) Assuming they are, are they possible as applied to actual sense-data? This seems to mean: *Can* any actual sense-data *be* compact series, or have parts which form a compact series? And maintains, p. 145, that they *can* be & must be composed of "mutually external units" = not parts of one another. Finally (3) he asks: Is there any reason to believe the world of sense "continuous"? And answers there isn't: but there's no reason why it shouldn't be.

But he never faces the question: What's meant by saying that a motion sensibly appears continuous? *Nor* the different question what's meant by saying that this sense-datum appears to be a continuous whole?

Even if he's right in saying that the sense-datum of a seen motion *may* be continuous in the mathematical sense, it doesn't in the least follow that what's meant by saying that it seems continuous is that it seems to be so. And I think it's certain it doesn't: so that we have to ask, with regard to quite a different sense of continuity: is it continuous in *that* sense?

He returns to the subject, again, *Anal. of Matter*, pp.279–282.[1]
And here again there seems to me to be the same lack of clearness.

He says (p. 279) "the philosophers' insistence that the Cantorian
continuum does not resolve their difficulties, are all derived from
this one puzzle, that a motion seems to consist of motions—or, as
Kant says, that a space consists of spaces".

He seems to want to say it doesn't.

And goes on (p. 280) "the continuity of the percept, they maintain, is quite obviously not that of the math. continuum, nor yet
the deceptive appearance of continuity wh. would exist if the
percept were a rapid staccato process". He says it *may* be either
one or the other.

But what does he mean? The continuity wh. the percept
actually has, or appears to have? But then *what* sort of continuity
does it *appear* to have?

The people he's arguing against say that it's not the property
of being or containing a compact series, which it appears to have;
& also that it *has* this other property. And R.'s statement that it
may be that it actually has that of the mathem. continuum, &
that it may be that it hasn't, is utterly irrelevant.

The question what's meant by saying that a motion or change
appears to be continuous is quite distinct from what's meant by
saying that a sense-datum appears to be a continuous spatial or
temporal whole: it's the latter question I want first to deal with;
& I'll return to the other afterwards.

What do we mean by saying that one thing A is "continuous
with" another thing B?

Whitehead, *Principles*, p. 102[2], says

"The concept of the continuity of nature arises entirely from
this relation of junction between events. Two joined events are
continuous one with the other." Cf. *Concept*, 76.[3]

He says then

"A is continuous with B" = "A is joined to B".

But what does he mean by "A is joined to B"?

I'm not going to give his actual definition, which is difficult
to follow; but I think I'm right in saying that it comes to this

[1] [B. Russell, *The Analysis of Matter* (London, 1927).]

[2] [A. N. Whitehead, *An Enquiry concerning the Principles of Natural Knowledge*
(Cambridge, 1919).]

[3] [A. N. Whitehead, *The Concept of Nature* (Cambridge, 1920).]

A is joined to B if & only if *either* (1) A "intersects" B or (2) A is "adjoined" to B.

And A intersects B if & only if *either* (1) A is a part of B *or* (2) B is a part of A (I think he also uses it so that, if A is identical with B) *or* (3) A & B have a common part.

W. actually gives as the def. of A "intersects" B, "A & B have parts in common": but he does this only because he assumes that *every* event has parts: *if* this assumption is true, then if A be a part of B, then A & B will have parts in common. But it's not certain that it is true; &, even if it were not, he would certainly wish to say that A & B do intersect if A is a part of B, so that it is better to define as I have done. It's certain that being a part of does not mean the same as being a common part, since the latter can only be defined in terms of the former.

W. is thus so using "continuous with" that, if A is a part of B, then A is continuous with B: but this does not seem to me to be in accordance with common usage. It seems to me the common & important usage of A is continuous with B is when it = A adjoins B.

The question is:

What does A "adjoins" B mean?

A adjoins B if & only if (1) A & B are "separated" (*Princs.*, p. 61) = R.'s mutually external = A & B do *not* intersect & (2) there is a third event C, such that (a) both A & B are parts of C & (b) C has no part which is separated both from A & from B. (McT., *N.E.*, p. 134).[1]

When 2 events are adjoined, they form "a set of parts" of some one event. What Broad calls "a set of adjoined parts" (p. 296).[2]

The important point here is the suggestion that "adjoined" is to be defined in terms of one particular relation of "part to whole" or "extending over": that to say A is adjoined to B does not merely mean that they have a relation to one another, but that they both have a relation to a third thing, wh. they compose; & to say they compose it doesn't mean that they *are* it & have certain relations to one another.

In other words to say that a sense-datum *is* continuous is to say that it's a peculiar sort of whole: one wh. has parts, but *is* not those parts: that it's a sort of whole which isn't a collection, nor a fact, *nor* a series.

---

[1] [J. McT. E. McTaggart, *The Nature of Existence*, vol. I (Cambridge, 1921).]

[2] [C. D. Broad, *The Mind and its Place in Nature* (London, 1925).]

⟨There's nothing to prevent it having parts which *do* form a series, & a compact series. But that's not what we mean by saying that it is or appears to be continuous. What we do mean is merely that it is a familiar sort of whole.⟩

It seems to me quite evident that our sense-data, many of them, have parts but that they are not identical with any collection of their parts or any series formed of their parts; & that very often they are composed of many different sets of parts, which we can't discriminate.

It's very important to distinguish this sense of whole & part (as McT. doesn't do) from that in which a member of a group is a part of that group. *This* sense of part is *not* transitive. And also from the relation of class-inclusion, which is transitive.

Thus to say: this appears continuous with that = there *is* a whole of this sort, such that this & that appear to make *it* up.

And to say this appears to be a continuous whole, is to say there is a whole of that sort such that this appears to be identical with it.

I think, therefore, there's no doubt that sense-data are continuous in the sense that they are *wholes* of a peculiar sort—*not* collections, *nor* facts, *nor* series.

But is the physical phase which a sense-datum represents certainly *not* continuous?

If it is a collection of electrons & nuclei or their surfaces then it is *not* continuous; and for all I know there may be some reason for saying that it is that. But I don't know what they are. Might it not be that all the scientific arguments shew is that phases of electrons & nuclei are *contained* in it, not that they are it? and that there is *not* empy space between them?

So far as I can see, corr. s. d., though continuous, *may* always be identical with what they represent, bec. what they represent *may* be so too.

What is certain is that two corr. s. d. may form one continuous whole, although the phases they represent do not.

Our whole visual field at any one time forms *one* continuous whole.

This, it seems to me, gives one very fundamental sense of continuity, which can't be defined in terms of math. continuity. I don't see how it can be denied there is such a sense.

There may be others. What's meant by saying a motion "seems continuous"? I can't tell.

VIII

IDENTITY AND PLACES

(1) That we do sometimes see a physical surface double—have a "double image" of one.

(2) That when we do thus see a surface P, then (as the name implies) we do really directly perceive 2 sense-data which are distinguished from all the other sense-data we're perceiving at the moment by the fact that they and they alone have to P a relation, such that if we hadn't been directly perceiving any sense-datum which had that relation to P, we shouldn't have been seeing P at all.

(3) That the relation expressed by saying that each is "an image of" P is precisely the same as that which I have expressed by saying of a corr. s. d. that it "represents" a certain surface.

From these premisses it will absolutely follow that the relation "represents" can't be identity.

I want to examine these, as usual, not only for the sake of the argument they jointly make, but for their own intrinsic interest.

(1) is quite certainly true. I want to note about it only (a) the epistemological point that it can't be true unless there are physical objects; & that we can't know it to be true unless we know there are. Many philosophers calmly use this arg. from double images while denying both;

& (b) that, in asserting it, I make no assertion as to whether we are "seeing" the physical surface, in the same sense as when we see one single. It *may* be held that the sense of "see" is different, whether it is or not partly depends on the truth of the other premisses.

(2) is the premiss which raises the most interesting points.

Many philosophers are not really convinced that it is true: they think it may be the case that we don't really have 2 sense-data, each of which is an "image" of P, but that what this arg. takes to be 2 entities is really only P itself; & that why it seems as if there were 2, is because P appears to be in 2 different places at the same time: they say P sensibly "appears to be 2" but isn't really.

I'm sorry to say I can't give actual examples. I can only give examples of people arguing against the view.

Thus Stout says (British Academy, 1905) "I look at a candle-flame . . .".[1]

S. says this is plainly nonsense; but he would not have troubled to say so, unless he thought some people held it.

But he does suggest a sort of argument when he says "one of which moves, while the other is unmoved"; & when he says "each has a positive nature". I.e. the only sort of arg. wh. can be used, i.e. that "this" has a pred. incompatible with what that has.

The truth is it's frightfully difficult to state it at all without begging the question.

You talk of "the one" & "the other", &, of course, you're then assuming that there are 2.

It can only really be done by taking a particular instance.

You see a whole that looks like that.

You can pick out A; you can pick out
B: is it really possible that B is the *same* as A?

In this particular instance we know it isn't because we know that A represents one part of the blackboard's surface, & B another, & that A does *not* represent the part wh. B represents. (We *do* know that: I don't say that's the only reason.)

But in the case of a double image we don't know this. Sometimes we think, falsely, that A does represent one that B doesn't; sometimes, when we know that it is a double image, we don't.

Is it possible that sometimes, when you have an appearance like this, A should be other than B, sometimes not?

Stout says: A & B can't be identical because A moves & B doesn't.

And, at first, this looks very conclusive: but there are 2 reasons why it isn't.

(1) Is it true that A moves, & B doesn't? Perhaps, only that A appears to me to move & B appears to me to be at rest. I.e. he is assuming that sense-data actually have the qualities they appear to have. This may be doubted, & make a difference.

(2) He says each with its own *positive* nature; & being "un-

---

[1] ["Things and Sensations". Reprinted in G. F. Stout, *Studies in Philosophy and Psychology* (London, 1930). See especially pp. 154 ff.]

moved" is *not* positive. What his argument rests on is that A has a certain character, B another & that these are incompatible.

But even if we grant they really have them, this isn't conclusive for 2 reasons.

Even if neither appears to move, A will always appear to have a certain character & B another, e.g. being to right & left of C; being at this distance & that distance from D.

Is it really impossible that a given thing at a given time should be *both* moving up & down & at rest, *both* to the right of C & also to the left of C, *both* at the distance D^1 from E & also at the different distance D^2 from E, *both* completely surrounded by red & also completely surrounded by black?

Suppose your thing is the sensible colour white: the sensible colour, white, certainly does, in a perfectly plain sense, move up & down in one part of your visual field while it is at rest in another; it certainly is both to the right of C & to the left; both at this distance D^1 from E & at this other.

Of course, there are people who deny this: who would say it's not the *same* colour which is both here & there: but that's a view which certainly can't be proved, & all appearances are against it.

Of course, this is only possible because the thing in question can be in 2 different places at the same time: but, then, in a perfectly obvious sense, colours *can*.

It really is impossible that x should be *both* moving here now & also at rest here now; but not at all impossible that x should be moving *here* now, & at rest *there* now.

If, then, this is possible, in the case of a colour or other quality, how are you to shew that it's impossible in the case of this sense-datum? Why shouldn't this be both here & there?

Of course, if, as some say, this sense-datum *is* a quality, it would follow that it can.

But even if it isn't, why shouldn't a sense-datum resemble a quality in this respect? How are you to prove that it can't?

I *think* the *first* answer is this.

If you consider what's meant by saying white is *to the left of* C, you find it is analysable into $(\exists x) \cdot x$ is white $\cdot$ x is *to the left of* C; & to the *right of* C into $(\exists x) \cdot x$ is white $\cdot$ x is *to the right of* C: and that the latter relations are relations which it is really impossible that the same thing should have to C at the same time. In the same way, if you analyse "white is in 2 different places now", this $= (\exists x,y) . x$ is white . y is white . x & y are *in 2 different* places: where the latter relation is necessarily aliorelative $=$ separated & not adjoined $+$ something positive (i.e. not merely *mutually external*).

It is this second sense of "in 2 different places" which R. is supposing to exist, & is calling being "outside of", when he says (*Arist. Proc.*, 1911–12, p. 17)[1] "it is in virtue of these self-evident properties that the numerical diversity of the 2 patches of white is self-evident. They have the relation of being outside each other, & this requires that they should be two, not one . . . It follows from this that the terms of spatial relations cannot be universals or collections of universals, but must be particulars capable of being exactly alike & not numerically diverse".

⟨There are aliorelative spatial relations; such a relation, it is logically possible, may hold between a & b, in spite of the fact that a is exactly like b; therefore in that case a & b are not universals; therefore the terms of these aliorelative spatial relations never are.⟩

But you have to add that the sense in wh. this sense-datum is to the left of C is the fundamental one, which is incompatible with its being at the same [time] to right of.

And how are you to prove (1) that there are these fundamental relations, (2) that it is these & not the others which hold between sense-data?

R. begins by assuming that this & that *are* two.

But suppose somebody says to him: There are *not* 2 patches; there are 2 places; & it's the same patch which is in both. What can he answer?

What he appears to answer is, in substance, pp. 14–15, that the objector might be right, if perceived space was absolute $=$ absolute positions were among objects of perception. But that this is not so; & therefore it must be that A & B are 2.

Though this is not how he puts it: he puts it as if A & B *themselves* might be a "whiteness in this place", or "whiteness in that" ("complexes of which this place & that place are respectively constituents", p. 10, p. 15).

And says (10 to 11) if we reject absolute position, it will become imposs. to distinguish the 2 as 2, unless each is an *instance* [of whiteness].

---

[1] ["On the Relations of Universals and Particulars". Reprinted in B. Russell, *Logic and Knowledge* (London, 1956).]

But why?

Why shouldn't places, which aren't absolute places, do as well?

It seems to me certain we can give a definite meaning to "this place is different from that", & hence to "these are 2 places", without supposing absolute places to be perceptible.

Take this sense-datum. We have the idea of being at this distance in this direction from it; & in that at that; & to say that a thing *might* be related in these 2 different ways to it is to say, these *are* 2 different places—2 different positions wh. it's possible for it to occupy. Anything which did occupy both would be in 2 different places.

I want to try to put in a precise form the argument I was giving, when I stopped, against those who say that, when we are directly perceiving a sensible whole like this, we really can distinguish 2 different *places* & see that A is in one, & B in the other, but that in spite of that it is quite possible that A is the very same sense-datum as B: that A & B are not 2.

We saw R. seemed to imply that we couldn't possibly distinguish a *place* in which A is from a *place* in which B is, without distinguishing A & B themselves as 2, unless *absolute* places were directly perceived.

But it isn't obvious he's right in this.

It certainly is possible in a sense that the places where A & B are should exist & be capable of being distinguished, even if A & B did not exist.

Take this definition of: "There are 2 places"

= "There is an entity, z, & a pair of spatial relations, R & S, such that if x had R to z & y had S to z then x & y would necessarily be in 2 different places".

This definition is not circular, since what is meant by "A & B are in 2 different places" is certainly an ultimate indefinable relation, *not* defined in terms of places.

This gives a sense in which there can be places where nothing is; just as there can be empty times.

And if this is right, if you can distinguish z & the relations R & S, then you can distinguish places, quite apart from A & B.

It looks, therefore, at first sight as if you *can* distinguish 2 places in this way, & as if, since you can, it's perfectly possible that the same sense-datum should be in both of them.

But now my def. says

R & S must be such that if x had R to z & y had S then x & y would necessarily be in different places. I.e. such that

xRz . ySz *entails* x & y are in different places.

This is obviously correct: there obviously couldn't be 2 places, unless if one thing were in the one, & another in the other, they would be in different places.

But the point which people fail to notice is that

xRz . ySz *entails* x & y are in different places

can only be true if R & S are *incompatible*, i.e. if xRz *entails* $\sim$(xSz).

This is brought out by the fact that if z could at the same time be here as well as there (which is what our people are supposing to be logically possible) then the fact that x had R to z, & y had S to z, would *not* entail that x & y were in different places: they might both be *here*.

The place defined as that in which anything would be wh. had R to z can't therefore be different from that defined as that in which anything would be wh. had S to z, unless R & S are incompatible: & to say that they are so is just to say that the same thing *can't* at the same time both have R to z & also have S to z.

There would not, therefore, be different places at all in a directly perceived spatial whole, unless these were *incompatible* spatial relations.

And the only kind there can be must be spatial relations between sense-data, since *none* of those between universals are incompatible with one another: the same universal might at the same time be in every place in this field.

Accordingly, any pair of spatial relations between sense-data which are such that from the fact that x & y had them to the same sense-datum it would follow that x & y were in different places, *must* be incompatible relations.

Hence if A is to left of C & B to right, A & B *can't* be the same.

I don't suppose this argument is really conclusive; but I think it's worth while giving it, because it's so important to call attention to the question what's meant by saying that the place where A is or appears to be is in any case a different place from that in which B is or appears to be. It certainly is; and, since A & B certainly are sense-data, if A really is in the one place & B in the other, A & B are certainly different.

But of course this doesn't prove the view wrong which says that A is the same as B & that it only *appears* to be in one or both of the 2 places.

You can often be quite certain that 2 things wh. you're perceiving in the same specious present *do* differ in colour, or length, or pitch etc.; but you never can be quite certain of any 2 that they *don't* differ in the very least degree—that they are *exactly* alike: even where you can't see that they differ, there may always really be some difference—some imperceptible difference.

This is assuming that sense-data really have the qualities they sensibly appear to have. As I say, this doesn't seem to me quite certain. But let's first assume that's true.

If it is true, then it seems to me there's no doubt whatever about the first part: you can often be quite certain that A is longer than B, or different in colour, or different in pitch.

But I would call attention to a passage in Johnson which seems to imply the denial of this: I don't think he can really intend to deny it: but if it's true, then what he says must be false. (II. 176,179.)[1]

He begins by asking: What do we mean by the question, *or how can we test*, whether one given line ... is greater or less than another?

Here he's probably talking of *physical lines*; but what he says ought to apply to sense-data as well.

He says relation of part to whole *entails* greater & less; & then goes on "if M & N are coexclusive" (= Whitehead's separated) then "in order to *compare their magnitudes*" we must be able to find parts of M that can be equated to one another as also to parts of N.

That is to say, in order to see that M is greater than N, we must be able to find a part of M *exactly equal* to a part of N!

He then goes on to say that we want "a *test* or definition of equality among unit parts"; and his conclusion is that there is "no literally logical justification for asserting equality or inequality" (p. 177): app. that we never *do* know anything to be exactly equal to anything else.

If not, & if to know one thing to be greater, we must know a

---

[1] [W. E. Johnson, *Logic*, Part II (Cambridge, 1922).]

part to be equal, it will follow that we never can be certain that one thing is greater!

This seems to me to be quite absurd. Perhaps he's confusing *comparing* with *measurement* & saying we never can be quite certain how much greater.

It seems to me quite certain that in order to know that M is greater than N, we don't need to know that anything we can *pick out* is exactly equal to anything else we can pick out.

If M is greater than N, it does follow that there is *a* part of M exactly equal to N: & perhaps this is part of the *meaning* of greater than. But we certainly don't need to be able to *find* any part of M of which we can say this is exactly equal to N.

So p. 179 he says, talking of stretches of hue or pitch: "I can see no *sense* in which they can be compared unless we have a test of equality".

Apparently he means that the difference between scarlet & Cambridge blue can't be seen to be greater than the difference between 2 shades of scarlet, unless we can say the difference between these 2 shades of scarlet is exactly equal to the difference between these!

This seems to me perfectly absurd.

The positive part is therefore quite certain; unless you say that all you can be quite certain of is that it sensibly appears to you to be greater.

But how about the negative?

Can't we ever say: This sense-datum is exactly the same length as that? This is exactly the same shade as that etc.?

This is a question about which there is a real difference of opinion.

Some people will say: Of these *physical* lines it is true: you can't ever tell that that's exactly the same length as that.

But of the sense-data it's different: that "of same length" = "not different in length", & that in the case of sense-data "not different in length" = "not *perceptibly* different (distinguishable) in length"; not different in colour = not perceptibly different in colour. In general that "different in colour" = "distinguishable in colour", & "indistinguishable" = not different.

And as to this I must own I feel uncertain: if I can't *see* any difference in colour between 2 sense-data, can there be any difference? or in length?

That 2 sense-data which are indistinguishable, in a certain respect, may nevertheless be different is one of the things R. is keen on maintaining: *Ext. World* p. 141, "two sense-data may be, & *must* sometimes be, really different when we can't perceive any difference between them". The "must" refers to Stumpf's argument. So *Analysis of Matter*, pp. 280–281, "We are compelled to infer a difference between A & B where we can't see any". "The relations between percepts are sometimes percepts sometimes not".

The question is: In the case of sense-data, isn't the statement: This is indistinguishable in respect of colour from that (= *I* can't distinguish them) identical with "This is exactly the same colour as that"?

If "different" = "distinguishable", they will be.

We can't say it's perfectly evident that sense-data *may* be different, where we can see no difference.

Stumpf's argument is supposed to *prove* that sometimes, where we can see no difference, they *are* different.

But it may be doubted whether it does.

(α) So far as I can see the argument depends on making an assumption, which can't be proved & is uncertain, about the relation of stimuli to sense-data.

You have 3 tuning-forks, A, B, C; tuned so as to give slightly different sets of vibrations.

You first sound A & B in quick succession; & you can't distinguish in respect of pitch between α, the sense-datum yielded by A, & β, that yielded by B.

You then sound B & C in quick succession, & you can't distinguish between β', the sense-datum *now* yielded by B, & γ that yielded by C.

You then sound A & C in quick succession, & you *can* distinguish between α' & γ'.

Now you haven't compared α with γ, nor β with γ, nor β' with γ' (& haven't *got* that β indistinguishable from γ, nor that α distinguishable from γ).

What the argument assumes is that α is not only indistinguishable from, but *not different* from α'; β from β'; γ from γ'. And the *only* reason for this is that the stimuli are the same. This may be highly probable; but I don't see how it can be quite certain. Isn't it possible that γ' is really distinguishable from γ, just because γ was produced immediately after a tone produced by B, & γ' immediately after one produced by A? The difference in the preceding stimulus *might* cause a difference in the effect produced by C, i.e. γ' might be different from γ, just because of its accompaniments.

(β) But the argument may be attacked on another ground.

Assuming that α & α', β & β', γ & γ', really are *not* different, it may be said that R.'s arg. (*Ext. W.*, p. 142) is invalid for the following reason.

He says β & β' *must* be different in pitch from α & α', because, *if* they weren't, they would be *distinguishable* from γ & γ', which they aren't; and also different in pitch from γ & γ', because, if they weren't, they would be distinguishable from α & α'.

This is to assume that if x & y are *not* different, & x & z are distinguishable, then y & z must be distinguishable.

But suppose different = distinguishable.

Then the argument is certainly invalid.

For the admitted facts of the case are

α & β not distinguishable, α & γ distinguishable, β & γ *not* distinguishable.

The argument assumes that indistinguishable does *not* entail *not* different; & this is certainly true for physical things. But *is* it true for sense-data?

THE REPRESENTATIVE THEORY
OF PERCEPTION

Only 3 tenable views as to use of "this" in "This is part of the surface of a blackboard".

(1) says

There is *some* relation, R, such that

"This is part of the surface of a blackboard"

= The thing to which *this* s. d. has R is part of the surface of a blackboard

= There is something to which alone this s. d. has R & which is part of the surface of a bl.

Views of this type will differ acc. to the view they take as to *what* relation or what sort of relation satisfies the above conditions.

But they may also differ, in an important way, acc. as they hold that *the* thing to wh. the corr. s. d. has R is or is not a *group* or *collection* of things.

(2) says

There is *some* relation, R, such that

"This is part of the surface of a blackboard"

= There are more things than one, to wh. this s. d. has R, & *the* things to wh. it has R (= the collection wh. has for members all the things wh. have R to it & has no other members) are taken collectively part of the surface of a blackboard.

Here again there are differences, according to the view taken as to what relation or what sort of a relation R is.

I'm going to deal with (1) & (2) together, as Type II, bec. the difference between them does not seem to me to be very important.

I want to say something about the relation of these views Type I, Type II & Type III[1] to "Common Sense".

This seems to me to be a subject about wh. it's important to get clear, & about which most philosophers are very far from clear.

[1] [Type I = direct realism; Type III = phenomenalism. Cf. "A Defence of Common Sense". Reprinted in G. E. Moore, *Philosophical Papers* (London, 1959).]

Most philosophers talk as if "Comm. Sense" took sides in this controversy; & as if, in saying this, they were saying that "we" all constantly think the one or the other—*we* all, including the plain man.

Thus Hume asserts that "we" all always take Type I—all think that our sense-data *are* material things; & Broad asserts the same on p. 1 of *Perception, Physics & Reality*[1]: "we think that what we perceive ⟨where his phrase "what we perceive" = "the corr. s. d."⟩ is the tree . . . except that what we perceive may be only a part of the tree", i.e. a part of its surface.

It seems to me that there's an ambiguity wh. it's very important to clear up in the way in wh. "Comm. Sense" is used.

I don't think it's true that "we" all do in fact take any view at all on the question to which Type I, II & III are answers: "Comm. Sense" in one, & the most important of its senses, takes no view at all on this subject; it simply doesn't raise the question.

What it *does* take a view on is that (1) "That's a blackboard" is often true, (2) that you & I often both see the same things, (3) that material things are continuants, & exist when none of us is seeing them, (4) that they really have shape & colour.

In short, I think we may say, just those things wh. are pre-supposed in saying that there is a "we" at all—that there is such a thing as Common Sense at all.

These are not merely Common Sense beliefs: they are things wh. we all know to be true.

It's only in quite another sense that we can say that C.S. takes or implies any view on the question to wh. these Types of view are answers.

All that we can say is, I think, that some of these views *would* appear more natural—less paradoxical than others—to any plain man who could understand the question.

In fact, the sort of thing I said in my def. of sense-data[2]: it is *natural*, at first sight, if you raise the question, to think that when you say "That is part of the surface of a blackboard" it is the s. d. that you're declaring to be so. In this sense, & this sense only, it may I think be said that Type I is a Com.S. view: *not* that we

[1] [C. D. Broad, *Perception, Physics, and Reality* (Cambridge, 1914).]
[2] [Cf. "A Defence of Common Sense".]

all do think it—we simply don't—but that anyone who understood the question would have a tendency to say "Yes"—the view would seem natural.

In this sense, & this sense only, I think we can say that to think some view of Type II is true, is also *natural* to Com. Sense—though incompatible with I ⟨though *some* views of this type, e.g. Russell's, are paradoxical.⟩ This also is implied in my def. of sense-data—that it's very easy on reflection to see reasons for doubting that it is they that we know to be surfaces. It's easy to make a plain man take the view that what we know to be a surface is not the sense-datum itself, but something *of* which the s. d. is an appearance: provided the view is one wh. doesn't make the physical thing a *logical construction*, & also doesn't make it a collection of wh. its appearances are members.

In this sense, I think, C.S. is against Type III (Mill, for instance, acknowledges that it is) & certain forms of Type II; & I think a certain weight is to be attached to the fact that it is. But the position is a *totally* different one to that of Common Sense to the assertion that there are material objects etc.: i.e. to what is presupposed in saying that Common Sense exists.

Consequences of rejection of Type I & adoption of II or III.

(1) To suppose Type I false, is to suppose that there is a sense of "appearance" quite different from any wh. we've hitherto met with; & many philosophers constantly use "appearance", not indeed certainly in this sense (they can't do that, unless Type I is false), but as a name for having *the* relation wh., on this view, sense-data would have to the corresponding physical objects.

"Sensible appearances".

There are in any case "sensible appearances" of physical objects.

But on Type I, this only means that the surfaces of physical objects sensibly appear to different persons to have certain properties.

Nothing can be said to be *a* sensible appearance, except any fact wh. is the fact that they so appear, or (if there are such things) the mental events wh. are the appearings of this & that to some one.

Sense-data themselves *aren't sensible appearances*.

But on Type II & III, sense-data themselves *are* appearances: to be an appearance = either (1) to be a thing related to a physical thing in the way in wh. *these* are or (2) to be a thing *perceived* in the way in wh. s. d. are, & also so related.

Thus we might say that Type II is the view that what we are saying is "There is a thing of which this is an appearance & wh. is the surface of a blackboard".

Only what I've said *defines* what's here meant by appearance: to be an appearance of a thing, is to have the relation, whatever that may be, which sense-data have either (a) to the surfaces or (b) to the objects.

(2) On this view the sense in wh. we "perceive" s. d. is quite different from the sense in wh. we perceive surfaces of physical objects, or physical objects.

Thus it says 3 different senses of "perceive" as applied to objects, apart from those applicable to facts.

(3) The rejection of Type I commits us to "representative theory of perception" *or* Mill's view.

We're now going on to consider as well as we can whether Type II can be a true view; & I think I defined this too narrowly.

I.e. we've got either to find a relation, if this view be true, of wh. it's true that this s. d. has it to this surface or to every member of this surface & to nothing else, or else a relation of wh. it's true that this surface & nothing else has it to this s. d. or every member of this surface & nothing else has it to this s. d.

I think the one follows from the other: i.e. if there's a relation wh. this s. d. has to this surface & nothing else, then the converse of this relation will be a relation wh. this surface has to this s. d. & nothing else. But I'm not sure about this.

And now for a general remark about views of this type.

I think the *majority* of modern philosophers have held views about the relation of corr. s. d. to material things acc. to wh. it would follow that Type II is true. I say this bec. I think the majority have certainly not held I & certainly not held III. As for the Gks. I don't know: I don't know, e.g., that Plato & Aristotle didn't hold I, though I think the Epicureans didn't. And about the Schoolmen I don't know.

But though modern philosophers have held views according to wh. this must be the analysis, hardly any of them has told us at all definitely, & none, I think, definitely enough, what relation or what sort of relation they suppose R to be. Russell, so far as I know, is the first who has made a fairly definite suggestion as to what it might be; & this isn't definite enough. That people should hold views of this type, without troubling themselves as to the question what the relation is, seems to me rather a scandal—it's a mark of the very backward state of philosophy. Of course, it's possible the view should be true, even if we can't discover what the relation is: but we can't have any reasonable certainty that it is true, unless we can find some relation or kind of relation wh. it's plausible to suppose does hold.

I'm left therefore to guess as to the kind of relation wh. people may suppose to be the one in question, except in Russell's & Broad's case. And I'm going to consider all I can think of that people might think at all plausible.

We've got to remember that there are 2 criteria wh. a suggested relation must satisfy

(1) It must either be one of wh. we know with certainty that every corr. s. d. has got it to the phase of surface wh. it represents, or to every member of that surface ⟨& to *nothing else*⟩;

(2) This isn't enough; it must also be one of wh. it's plausible to suppose that whenever we make these judgments we are making a judgment about this relation, to the effect that this s. d. has it to one thing only, or only one thing has it to it.

I. And first of all I want to consider a suggestion wh. may seem plausible at first sight: namely, there seems to be a relation wh. *ex hypothesi* satisfies (1)—viz. the relation wh. I have called "representing". Why shouldn't we suppose that what we're saying is: The thing wh. this represents is a phase of part of the surface of a blackboard?

It is true that in the case of every corr. s.d. there is one & only one surface or collection of surfaces wh. it represents.

But I think the objection is that the relation is such that we don't know that there's only one *thing* ⟨particular or group⟩ to wh. the s.d. has this relation.

On views of Type II we only know that this represents one & only one thing, because we already know that it has some other relation, R, to one & only one thing.

II. The second kind of view I want to consider is views wh. say that R is to be defined partly at least in terms of "cause". It has, I think, been a view very commonly held in philosophy that we only know of physical objects as the things wh. stand in some causal relation to our sense-data.

One thing seems to me to be certain: namely that whenever I perceive a sense-datum wh. represents a physical surface, the fact that I perceive has for one among its causes the phase of surface in question. This seems to me a well-established psycho-physical prop.

But it's only my *perception* of the corresponding s.d. with regard to wh. it seems to me certain that it is causally connected in this way with the surface wh. I see: that the existence of the s.d. itself is so connected is of course doubtful: & yet it's only if the s.d. itself is caused to exist by the physical phase, that we can get any plausible view at all of R in terms of cause.

For it is, I think, practically certain that when we talk of that surface, we are not talking about our *perception* of the s.d., but only of the s.d. If, therefore, R is to be defined in terms of cause, the s.d. *itself* must stand in a causal relation to the surface.

This, therefore, must be assumed in any case to make any view of this type plausible; but I don't regard this as a fatal objection to the view that R can be defined partly in terms of cause, for I think it's possible that the s.d. itself really is caused in this way: I only want to emphasize that this is by no means certain, whereas it is certain that my perception of it is.

We assume then that the s.d. itself is caused by the phase it represents.

And hosts of philosophers, who ought to have known better, seem to me constantly to have talked as if we could simply describe the phase of surface as *the* thing which causes the s.d.

If it were the *only* cause of the s.d., then of course we might suggest that what we mean by "this surface" is "the thing which caused this s.d.", & that R = "caused". Though it's to be noted that, then, the prop. that this phase caused this sense-datum ceases to be a scientific prop., & becomes a mere tautology.

But what I want to insist on is that this def. certainly won't do; for the simple reason that even if this phase did cause this s.d., it's certainly not the *only* cause of it. It is for instance quite certain that a phase of my retina is also *among* its causes.

I ended by saying that by "that surface" we can't possibly mean "*the* cause of this sense-datum", for the simple reason that

that surface is certainly *not the* cause of this sense-datum, i.e.
its only cause: it's only at most one among its causes: all we know
for certain is that it's one among the causes of my perception of it.

But I didn't give my reasons; & it's important to consider them.
How do I know that it isn't *the* cause of this sense-datum?

Because I know that *one* of the causes of my perception of this
sense-datum is the occurrence of certain events in both my
retinae: I shouldn't be seeing this sense-datum now, *unless* my
retinae had been affected in a certain way just before; & events
in the surface of the blackboard only do cause my perception of
the sense-datum bec. they first cause my retinae to be affected
in that way. Moreover, we can not only say I shouldn't be seeing
it now, *but for the way* in which ⟨unless⟩ my retinae have been
affected, we are also, it seems, entitled to the prop. that, if my
retinae had been affected in just that way, then provided my
optic nerves & brain had been in the condition in wh. they were,
I should have seen just this sense-datum, even if the surface of
that blackboard had not existed.

But not only are events in my retinae just as much causes of
my perception of the sense-datum as events in the blackboard.
Also there are hundreds of others: e.g. first there are ever so
many events in the space between the blackboard & my retinae;
& also ever so many events in my optic nerves & brain.

All this seems to me to prove with certainty that events in the
blackboard are not *the* cause of my perception of this sense-
datum. But of course all these are only results of science, which I
personally take on trust, & they all assume the existence of
material things & our knowledge about them. It seems to me
astonishing how philosophers who profess to doubt of the existence of material things, yet constantly assume, in the very
arguments by which they profess to shew the doubtfulness of the
existence of material things, the certainty of such facts about the
retina & nerves & brain.

"That surface" then certainly not = "The cause of this
s.d.".

If, therefore, *any* view of this type is to be true, it must be
some view of the form "The thing wh. is cause of this s.d. &
also related to it in certain other ways", i.e. the *one* among its
causes which also possesses certain other peculiarities.

(a) What definition of R of this sort is it plausible to suggest?

What do we know to be true of this phase of surface, which is *not* true of other causes of this perception of mine?

One thing we know is that it is *the* one among the causes of this perception, which I am non-referentially *perceiving*: this is really true. I'm *not* perceiving either referentially or non-referentially any *other* of its causes, e.g. my retina.

But we certainly can't define "having to this sense-datum R" as = "both causing this sense-datum & perceived by me": because on views of type II, part of what is meant by "this phase is non-referentially perceived by me" is "I am directly apprehending a sense-datum to which this phase has R: i.e. non-referential perception is defined in terms of R, & therefore R can't be in terms of non-referential perception. This may not be the *whole* of what's meant by non-referential perception: the whole may be "I am non-referentially perceiving O" = "There is a sense-datum with regard to which I know that only one thing has R to it, & to which O has R".

(b) Take "The *primary* cause of this sense-datum". This is a phrase frequently used.

It looks at first sight as if in some sense or other events in the blackboard may really be the *primary* cause of my perception; or to use another phrase "*the source*".

The objection urged against *the* cause was that there were other causes intervening between the events in the blackboard wh. are causes & my perception; & we avoid these by suggesting that it is not *the* cause, but the *primary* one, i.e. earlier than any of those others.

But how can we possibly define "primary" cause in such a way that it will be true that they are the *primary* cause?

If we substitute *first* for "primary" = earliest in time, everyone would scout the suggestion that those are the *first* cause. Those events in the blackboard must themselves have had causes, certainly have in some cases: & cause is transitive, if A is cause of B, & B of C, then A is of C.

It seems certain, therefore, that if we mean by "primary" simply "earliest", the blackboard is *not* the primary cause of my perception; & very probable that there is no primary cause.

In order to get a tenable def. we should have to suppose that primary = the earliest among its causes wh. also satisfies *some other condition.* And though I'm not certain some such def. couldn't be found, I'm quite unable to suggest one.

(c) The most plausible suggestion I can think of, as to a relation partly definable in terms of "cause", wh. it may be maintained that the surface really always has to the corr. s.d. & nothing else has to it, is one just the opposite of this, viz. that it's the *latest* among its causes wh. satisfies certain other conditions. This does seem to me to be a really possible view.

This relation was suggested to me by certain passages in the writings of Broad: & I'm going to introduce it by reference to what he says, though as you'll see he isn't proposing to give an answer to our question. I dare say he would no longer think what he here says true; but it is worth quoting, bec. it is a sort of thing which I believe many philosophers would say, & which at first sight sounds very plausible. One thing it says is that we only know of physical objects as having a certain kind of causal relation to our sense-data.

Another reason I have for quoting it is that I want to bring out the connection between the question Broad is here trying to answer & our question—a connection wh. might easily be over-looked, since it looks as if the 2 questions had scarcely anything to do with one another. It seems to me, however, that any correct answer to Broad's question must mention a relation such that, if the answer is correct, (1) it always holds between any physical surface we see & any corr. s.d., & does *not* hold between anything else & that s.d. & (2) is such that in any case in wh. we know of the existence of any physical surface we are perceiving, we must *know* that it has this relation to the corr. s.d.

Mind, XXX [1921], p. 395.[1]

Broad asks: On the hypothesis that sense-data are not identical with the surfaces wh. they represent, what *right have we* to believe in physical objects?

And he answers that one fact which helps to give us a right, is that it *is* reasonable to suppose that certain series of successive sensa have *a common, relatively permanent, set of conditions.*

He implies *we should have no right*, unless it was *reasonable to suppose this.*

This *kind* of assertion has been often made, & it seems to me very difficult to see exactly what it amounts to.

[1] [C. D. Broad, "The External World".]

It isn't *reasonable to believe* in physical objects, unless *it's reasonable to suppose* this.

But there are steps here.

(1) B. must mean: Nobody believes *reasonably* in physical objects, unless *he* believes reasonably, in the case of some set of sensa, that they have a common permanent condition.

This isn't clear from the statement of the form: It isn't reasonable to believe in q, unless it's reasonable to believe in p.

This is partly a statement of a constitutive relation: q isn't true, unless p is true.

But it's clear in fact that it isn't reasonable for A to believe in q, in spite of the holding of this constitutive relation, unless A not only believes in p, but *reasonably* believes in p.

The fact that p is true, & q follows from p, & A believes p, doesn't make it reasonable for A to believe q, unless A *reasonably* believes p.

(2) If A knows p, it is reasonable for him to believe p (though not vice versa).

Hence if he can't *reasonably* believe q without *reasonably* believing p, he can't *know* q without *reasonably* believing p; & also obviously without knowing p.

Hence if B. is right, before we can *know*: This is a physical object; that is a physical object; we must know: This series of sensa has a common permanent condition.

Can it be that what we mean by: "This is a clock" the first time we do know this, is "*The* common permanent condition of this series of sensa is a clock"?

If not, it seems to me B. must be wrong: for otherwise, how could it be necessary that we should know: "This series of sensa has *a* common permanent condition" before we know: "This is a clock"?

Now this *can't* be what we know, unless the physical object is the *only* common permanent condition, or set of conditions, of such series of sensa as B. has described.

Is it? Our retinae aren't, because they are not conditions for tactual sensa. But our *brains* are. If tactual & visual sensations are localised in different parts of the brain, we might say that no part of the brain is a common permanent condition for both.

⟨Is the *only* physical object the *whole* of which is a common permanent condition.⟩

B. suggests (as many others, e.g. Ward, have) that before we know: This is a physical object, we must have known not only of a series of sensa of our own that they have a common permanent condition, but also of sensa of other people.

This would get over the brain difficulty; bec. *my* brain is not a condition for the sensa of other people.

But every such suggestion that our knowledge of physical objects requires a previous knowledge of mental facts about other people, is liable to the objection that (1) we seem to know of physical objects as early as we know of any such facts & (2) that it seems doubtful whether we *can* know of mental facts about other people before we know of the existence of their bodies, i.e. physical objects.

We must then say something like: The permanent condition of this set of sensa, which is common condition of them all.

I.e. of *all* the events wh. were causes of each of these sensa, there are certain sets, one from each, wh. were events in one permanent thing, & one such set consisted of events each of wh. was earlier in time than any event in another set that was a cause of the same sensa.

Does the physical object of which a set of sensa are all appearances, satisfy this condition?

I can't see that it mayn't: but it seems highly unplausible to suppose we know all this about a set of sensa before we know: This is a physical object.

However, this is as plausible as any view wh. defines R in terms of cause, wh. I can think of.

But there remains another objection.

We certainly often *believe* "That is a physical object", before we have had any series of successive sensa of *it*, & we *know* it too.

However what we mean by this can't always be "The common remote cause of this set of sensa is a physical object".

What else could we mean?

It may be urged we always do believe or know that under certain circumstances we *should* have certain sensa, & that what we are judging is that there's one & only one thing wh. is the earliest thing, wh. both is a cause of this & *would* be or would have been a cause of the other. ⟨Wh. both is a cause of this & would have been the earliest one of the other, if these had existed.⟩

This view that when we know: This is a physical object; we

always do know a set of props. to the effect, that, in certain circumstances, we should have had certain other sensa, is a view wh. we shall meet again—Mill's view is based on it; & one objection to it is that it seems as if, when we do know it, the circumstances involve facts about physical objects, in wh. case we must know of the existence of some physical objects without it.

This objection is *perhaps* not fatal.

But in the causal form there's another objection.

Namely we have to consider Broad's statement: Is it reasonable to suppose that sets of s.d. have a common permanent cause? He says we "need an explanation". Do we?

It seems to me it's only reasonable to suppose that so-&-so has a certain kind of cause, if (a) we observe it to have one & (b) we have in the past observed similar things to have one. Now we can't on this view *observe* such a series to have this for their common cause, because that they have this for their common cause is a tautology.

But it's only in the case of physical objects that we can observe a series of successive things to have a common permanent cause.

⟨Can it be true that our first knowledge "that is a physical object" is knowledge with regard to some sensa "there is one & only one permanent condition of this & other sensa, wh. is later than all other permanent conditions"?⟩

The latter part of what I said in my last lecture was very muddled.

We saw in the earlier part that this phase of this surface is certainly not the *only* cause of this sense-datum.

But I took certain statements of B.'s as suggesting that, if you consider certain *series* of successive sense-data, instead of a single sense-datum, there may be something or other which is the *only* relatively permanent condition *common* to them all.

(B.'s language about this is rather vague. *Sci. Th.* p. 275 suggests that there is *only* one relatively permanent *set* of conditions, common to them all if they're all visual; but p. 276 suggests that where some are tactual & some visual "it is natural to suppose that there is *something* (not some *set* of conditions) common & relatively permanent which accounts for the predominant agreement in shape between the visual & tactual sensa". And I don't think there's any real reason for this distinction between the 2 cases, of a *set* of conditions in the one, & a *single* condition in the other.)

Let's take the case where you look at the same surface of a penny from many different distances & many different directions.

Is there any sense at all in which the surface in question is the *only* relatively permanent condition, *common* to all the different visual sense-data; i.e. which is a causal condition of them all?

Obviously not literally; because my body is so, *if* the surface is so: i.e. if it's not only my perception of the sense-data, but the sense-data themselves that are caused.

But I think what B. was really thinking of was: the *only* relatively permanent thing which *both* is a cause of all *these* sense-data, & *not* a cause of any of the other sense-data I have simultaneously. This cuts out my body, & also particular parts of my body like my retinae & my brain.

It think it's just possible that something like this really is true: i.e. that it's the only thing of which it is true that every one of the sense-data which represent that surface is caused by a phase of that thing, & also that it's *not* true that any of the other sense-data I have during the period is caused by a phase of it.

Why I brought in the "latest" common cause was because I didn't feel sure that there mightn't be a common cause of all these phases (e.g. the other parts of the penny) which would also satisfy this condition. But perhaps this is unnecessary.

What does seem to me plausible is that that surface *has* some causal relation to that series of sense-data, which nothing else has: though it's very difficult to formulate.

Assume that it has; we now come to a more difficult question still. Namely: is it plausible to suppose that, *in such a case*, what I mean by "that surface" is: The thing, of which a phase was cause of each of these sense-data, while no phase of it was a cause of any others that I had during the period?

This involves

(1) the question whether the facts B. points out *do by themselves* make it reasonable to suppose that there is such a common cause. And I can't help doubting whether they do. I can't help suspecting that why it seems reasonable, is solely because of the knowledge we have as to how physical things do behave: and that, hence, unless we had *other* reasons to believe in physical things, this would give us none.

But

(2) it doesn't directly give us an answer to the question what R is; since R is a relation which this *phase* has to me, *not* this surface. I suppose the answer would have to be this.

Let's call the sense-datum we're considering S. We're supposed to know that there's only one surface which was a common cause of S & certain other sense-data, & also *not* of any others that I had at the same time. The relation wh. this surface has to S is this complicated one: let's call it Q—a relation into the definition of which those other sense-data, or descriptions of them, enter.

Then *"the* thing which has R to S" will = *"the* phase of *the* thing which has Q to S, which was among the causes of S".

And R will be a different relation in each different case, since different sense-data will enter into the definition of Q in each different case.

(3) There are the cases, to which I referred last time, where we haven't had any series of sense-data. What do we mean here by "That surface"?

You just take one glance at a thing & say: "That surface".

This must mean, I think, something like: *"The* one among the causes of S, which *would* have been causing now sense-data of these kinds, under these conditions, & is *not* a cause of any sense-data I have now except S, & wouldn't under those conditions have caused any except of those kinds".

We do in fact know that it would have, if we know that the sense-datum *does* repr. a physical surface. Our knowledge about successive sense-data of the same thing does give us knowledge of what would have been the case.

And we can say we know this also in (2): that (2) gives us something equivalent to saying this.

The theory suggested by Broad wh. I discussed last time was that

"That is part of the surface of a clock"

= "The latest among the causes of this s.d. of wh. it is also true that, if I had been there, it would have been a cause of a s.d. of this kind, if my hand had been there, it would have been a cause of a s.d. of this kind, etc. etc., is the surface of a clock".

This or something like it seems to me the *only* account of R in terms of cause which can possibly be true; & it seems to me it may just possibly be true; but as it stands it does not, I think, seem very plausible.

I will merely state in order what seem to me to be the principal objections to it:

(1) That it requires that it should be true that the corr. s.d., & not merely my perception of it, *is* caused by events in that surface. It's certain my perception is but doubtful whether the s.d. is. And we can't mend it by saying "The latest among the causes of *my perception of* this s.d. etc.", bec. when I know "That is a physical surface" I am certainly *not* always knowing anything about my perception of the s.d. This is an objection to every causal theory, i.e. [one] wh. defines R in terms of cause.

(2) That it seems highly doubtful whether the first time a child knows "That's my hand" etc., he is knowing with regard to his s.d. any fact whatever wh. includes as a part that it has a cause; & doubtful also whether whenever we know such things we are knowing any such fact.

This is an objection to every causal theory.

(3) That the prop. "That phase is one among the causes of this s.d." does not seem to be a tautology; whereas on this view it would be since it would be "The one among the causes of this sense-datum wh. satisfies these conditions, is one among the causes of this sense-datum".

This is an objection to every causal theory.

(4) That it seems very doubtful whether the mere fact that a succession of sense-data have to one another the relations wh. a set of successive s.d. corr. to the same physical object sensibly appear to have does *by itself*, as B. seems to suppose, make it reasonable to suppose that they have a common cause: still less that, if this was our only evidence, we could *know* that they have. It seems, on the contrary, as if part of our evidence for the prop. that they have, consists in our knowing first that they *do* all corr. to the same surface, i.e. that they are all s.d. of the same object.

(5) That it seems very doubtful whether the hypothetical prop. doesn't involve a previous knowledge of physical objects.

On the whole, the view seems to me *so* doubtful that it's certainly worth while considering alternatives.

This is a theory which I'm inclined to think most likely to be true of any of Type II.

It consists in saying that R is a relation not to be identified with or defined in terms of any relation known to hold in any other cases except between sense-data & the physical surface to wh. they correspond; & unanalysable.

We might call it "being an appearance of" or "manifestation of"; & then say that this is ultimate.

"The thing of which this is an appearance".

We should have to say: we know, in certain cases, that there is one & only one thing of wh. a sensum is an appearance; & that we know this *directly* in many cases, not by inference *on the basis of past experience*. We cannot have learnt it by *experience*, because we have never *observed* such a relation to hold between any 2 things.

⟨I don't want to say that it mayn't be *inference* in some sense.

It is *because* of all the properties—the whole situation—wh. the sense-datum seems to have, that I know that it *is* round, or that the thing of wh. it is an appearance is so.

All that I say is that it's not because I've *found* by past experience that things wh. had those properties also had that of being round: because I never *can* have found that a thing was round in the sense in question.

You can say if you like that my view is that I know *intuitively* in certain cases that a sense-datum is an appearance of something else, & also that it has certain properties.

Some people feel a strong objection to theories of this type; & I own I myself feel very uncomfortable about it: that's why I've thought it worth while to go into others.

It is only by induction from past experience that I can know of the existence of objects wh. I don't observe, & what properties they have.

This seems a very plausible principle: & if you use "observe" in the sense in wh. it commonly applies in ordinary life, i.e. that sense in wh. you do observe physical objects, & that they have certain properties, I think it is true.

But why people object to the view I've just been suggesting, is that they have assumed, without enquiry, that what is true of observation in this first sense, is true also of observation in the sense in wh. it is applied to sense-data.

I *don't* (if Type I is to be rejected) *observe* physical objects in the sense in wh. I observe sense-data, nor do I (either on this view or on that of Type I) *observe* them to have properties, in the sense in wh. it is supposed that sense-data are observed to have them—i.e. that they appear to have them.

Suppose (on Type I) a penny looks to me round, & really is round: my knowledge that it is *round, may* be called "observation", but can't be *identified* with its looking round.

People suppose this must be inference on the basis of past experience.⟩

H

PART II

SELECTIONS FROM A COURSE OF LECTURES
GIVEN IN 1925-26

I

CLASSES AND INCOMPLETE SYMBOLS

One of the commonest ways in wh. we use "thinking of" is when we say S is thinking of so-&-so, where so-&-so is a *class* or collection or set of things—as e.g. S was thinking of the human race or of mankind, S was thinking of Woman (women in general), S was thinking of children, S was thinking of elephants, etc. etc. And it's natural to ask: Is this use of "thinking of" the same as that in wh. we use it of a real individual? Or in other words is the relation in wh. we stand to a class as a whole, when we think of it, the same as that in wh. we stand to a particular member of it, when we think of that member?

In considering this question, I think it's as well to begin by pointing out that there are 2 very different relations in wh. we may stand to a class, both of wh. are such that, if we stand in either, we should be said to be thinking of it.

Namely: (1) If I consider such a prop. as "All men are mortal" it follows that I am thinking of mankind—that is whenever I conceive a hypothesis expressed by "all" where *all* is used distributively, i.e. [all men are mortal] = every man is mortal. And (2) I can also consider such a prop. as "Mankind have already exceeded many millions in number", where we shall say that it is the same class we are thinking of, but where I am conceiving some hypothesis about mankind collectively: this can't be put in the form "Every man has exceeded many millions in number".

On the other hand, if I'm conceiving merely "Some men are red-haired", I don't think it would be natural to say that *ipso facto* I'm thinking of *men* or mankind.

Now it seems to me prob. that whenever we think of a class we are doing one or other of these 2 things; & probable that to say we're thinking of it *means* that we are.

Let's consider whether, if so, we have the same relation to the class, as to Broad.

(1) Take first what we may call thinking of it distributively.

It's quite certain here that we have an actual relation to every member of the class, wh. we haven't to anything *not* a member of it, consisting in the fact that we're conceiving a *certain sort of hypothesis* with regard to a predicate wh. applies to each of them & to nothing else. And one thing that's perfectly certain about the whole business, is that this relation wh. we have to *each* member is *not* one that can be called *thinking of*; & also I think that it can't be called a cognitive relation. It's perfectly certain that nobody ever does or can *think of* every man there's ever been at the same time; although he can have *this* relation.

But, of course, the fact that you have this relation to each of its members does constitute a relation (a different one) between you & the class as a whole; & it might be said that this relation is really identical with that wh. you have to an individual, or with *one* of those meant by "thinking of" as applied to an individual.

But it certainly can't be unless both (1) an individual is himself a class & (2) one of the things you mean by "thinking of" an individual, is conceiving, with regard to some predicate wh. determines the class of things wh. is the individual, some prop. or hypothesis of the form "Everything wh. has this predicate . . .". Even if (1) is true, it would by no means follow that (2) is so too; & it seems to me extremely unlikely that (2) is ever true. For my part I don't think (1) is true either, although there are a good many philosophers who would say that Broad & this desk *are* classes.

(2) Take next the relation we have to a class when we think of it *collectively*; i.e. when we conceive with regard to it some prop. of the form "Mankind as a whole numbers many millions" or "has me for a member". Can it be that this relation is identical with any wh. we mean by "thinking of" as applied to Broad?

What kind of relation have we to mankind when we conceive a prop. of this sort?

In trying to answer this question, I must, I think, try to explain the view with regard to classes put forward by Russell & Whitehead in *Principia*, vol. I, pp. 75–80, 196–198[1]; & which has also been explained by Russell in *Introd. to Math. Philosophy*, pp. 181–184, & in *Monist*, July 1919, *The Philosophy of Logical Atomism*[2]: I don't know whether this view is true or not; but I think it may be true, & the mere possibility that it may be is very important. It seems to me that the understanding of this possibility is of

---

[1] [A. N. Whitehead and B. Russell, *Principia Mathematica*, 3 vols., 1st ed. (Cambridge, 1910–13).]

[2] [Reprinted in B. Russell, *Logic and Knowledge* (London, 1956).]

fundamental importance for philosophy. And though it's extremely difficult to understand fully, I think everybody who does Metaphysics should try to understand it.

I talk of *"the view"*; but in fact there are a good many different views, not all necessarily connected with one another; & one of my objects is to separate them out.

I think the best point to begin with is the analysis wh. R. & W. give as being, *possibly*, the correct analysis of absolutely *every* prop. in which anything is asserted of a class as a whole—of a class collectively.

The exact formula is this:

$$f\{\hat{z}(\psi z)\} . = : (\exists \phi) : \phi ! x . \equiv_x . \psi x : f\{\phi ! \hat{z}\}$$

And we can best understand this by taking a particular example.

Let $\hat{z}(\psi z) =$ the Apostles & let $f =$ were twelve in number.

Then what this asserts is

The Apostles were twelve in number $= (\exists \phi) : \phi ! x . \equiv_x .$ x was an Apostle : $\phi ! \hat{z}$ is 12 in number.

There's one point in this, that's irrelevant for our purposes, & wh. I don't propose to try to explain: viz. what is meant by $\phi !$, in $\phi ! \hat{z}$. This means that $\phi ! \hat{z}$ is a particular sort of propl. function, wh. R. calls predicative: & this, in my language, means the same as that it is a particular sort of predicate.

Apart from this, it's easy to see what the statement amounts to:

It says: The Apostles were 12 in number

$=$ There's a predicate *coextensive* with the pred. "is an Apostle", wh. was 12 in number.

This, you see, is not the same thing as saying that the pred. "is an Apostle", has the number 12; although that is something wh. follows from it.

And you can see one reason why it seems to be at all events more like what we do mean by "the Apostles were 12 in number" than would be "the predicate "is an Apostle" is 12 in number".

The reason I mean is this. That the predicate "is an Apostle" is 12 in number, or applies to 12 things, is a prop. which nobody could know without having this predicate directly before his mind. Whereas it's obviously possible that with regard to the actual set of men who were Apostles, somebody should have known that *they* were 12 in number, without ever having formed the conception of being an Apostle, & *a fortiori* without knowing that these & these alone were Apostles. E.g. a person might have seen all the Apostles in a room together, & counted them, & found out that they were 12, & he would have then known, with regard to the class, wh. is in fact determined by the pred. "is an Apostle", that it was 12 in number, even though he did not know that the pred. was 12 in number. In other words, we have to allow for the patent fact that we use class in such a sense that 2 different people may both be knowing or conceiving with regard to the *same* class that it has a certain number, although the defining pred. by wh. one refers to the class is quite different from that by wh. the other refers to it. And it seems fairly plausible to say that when *I* say of somebody else: S knew that the Apostles were 12 in number, I am saying something like $(\exists \phi) : \phi$ is coextensive with "is an Apostle" : S knew that ϕ applied to 12 things. This, however, is not exactly what R.'s formula would seem to imply. It is rather $(\exists \phi) : \phi$ is coextensive with "is an Apostle" : S knew $(\exists \chi) . \chi$ is coextensive with $\phi . \chi$ is 12 in number.

Suppose the defining pred. by wh. I refer to a given class is "is a man" & that by wh. another refers to the same class is "is a featherless biped". R.'s interpretation does not get over the difficulty that the actual fact I'm knowing when I know this is different from what S is knowing. I shall be knowing, say, "There is a predicate ϕ coextensive with "is a man" wh. numbers more than a million"; while he'll be knowing: "There is a predicate ϕ coextensive with "is a featherless biped" wh. numbers more than a million." All that R. does, so far as I can see, is to secure that we should both have an indirect cognitive relation to each of a set of other facts, wh. is the same in both cases: to every fact, namely, wh. is a fact with regard to a pred. coextensive with either of our two, that that pred. applies to more than a million things. If you know that there is at least one pred. coextensive with ϕ, wh. has the number 12, you have an indirect cognitive relation to each such fact if there are several: & if χ is coextensive with ϕ, then anybody who knows this of χ, has the same indirect cognitive relation to each such fact. Whereas if all you knew, respectively, was χ has number 12, & ϕ has the number 12, even though these were coextensive, each of you would have no *cognitive* relation to any *same* fact. R. does not secure that there's any *one* fact to wh. you both have the same cognitive relation, but he *does* secure that there's *either* this or a set to each of which you have this.

identity ?

Principia, p. 75.

(1) Symbols for classes, = symbols like $\hat{z}(\phi z)$, will be incomplete symbols; & says this means "their *uses* are defined, but they themselves are not assumed to *mean* anything at all. That is to say, the uses of such symbols are so defined that, when the *definiens* is substituted for the *definiendum,* there no longer remains any symbol wh. could be supposed to represent a class".

Take the formula: there *does* remain a symbol which takes the place of $\hat{z}(\phi z)$ but nobody would say that it represents a class.

Why not? Because the form of combination of $f\{\hat{z}(\phi z)\}$ suggests that $\hat{z}(\phi z)$ is the subject of this prop., whereas it turns out that it's a predicate.

This is the best I can do, by way of explaining what this particular view of R. comes to.

Let's now try to apply it to our particular problem of *thinking of* a class collectively.

According to this view what I am doing is always thinking with regard to some particular pred., which defines or determines the class in question, that there are one or more preds., coextensive with this one, wh. possess the pred. in question; & I think I must be knowing or at least reasonably believing that there are.

E.g. if I think with regard to the class of distinguished living philosophers that it has Broad for one of its members, I am thinking that there is some pred., coextensive with that of being a distinguished living philosopher, wh. has Broad for one of its members.

Thus to say that I'm thinking of the class would be to say that I have a certain peculiar relation to a certain pred. wh. determines the class; the relation being that I'm knowing with regard to it that there is a pred. coextensive with it.

Thus, if this analysis were true, it would seem to follow that I can't possibly have the same relation to a class as to Broad—unless Broad is himself a class.

So much for that: the prop. that *every* prop. wh. is a prop. about a class taken collectively is to be analysed in this way, seems to me to be a perfectly clear prop. But I said this isn't *all* R. says; & I want now to discuss the other things he says.

R. himself uses the following language (*Principia,* p. 75):

He says that $\hat{z}(\phi z)$, as he uses it, is an "incomplete symbol"; & that hence, if in *every* prop. which is about a class taken collectively, the symbol which "represents" the class (or is a symbol *for* a class) taken collectively is used in the same way, i.e. the analysis of the whole prop. is that given, then symbols wh. "represent" classes taken collectively are all of them "incomplete symbols".

But he talks further, p. 75, as if, supposing "symbols for classes" or "symbols wh. represent classes" are incomplete symbols, these classes themselves are incomplete symbols: (p. 75) "an extension (wh. is the same as a class) is an incomplete symbol". And later "leads to the non-introduction of classes except as incomplete symbols".

This is very confusing because he goes on to say, that, supposing his analysis is true, then classes are "fictitious objects", "not genuine objects", "symbolic fictions", "logical fictions" (elsewhere "logical constructions"); & that to say this implies that "there are no classes".

The identification of "classes are logical fictions" with "classes are incomplete symbols" occurs also in *Introd.*, p. 182.

So also *Monist* (April 1919), p. 222: "There are a great many other sorts of incomplete symbols. There are classes . . . Such aggregation of symbols are *really* the same thing as what I call "logical fictions" ".

But in *Monist*, pp. 353 & 359, he says something very different.

"You will have to say that in the sense in wh. there are particulars, in that sense it is *not true* to say that there are classes. The sense in wh. there are classes is a different one from the sense in wh. there are particulars."

(P. 359.) "It is not significant to say there are such things as classes."

This seems to me to be all in the highest degree confusing.

You see, he says

If my analysis is correct

then (1) There is a sense of "There are" such that "there *are* classes" will be true.

(2) But there's another sense of "There are such things as classes" in wh. this will be *false*.

(3) There's a sense of "There are" such that the expression "There are classes" will mean nothing at all, i.e. will express neither anything true, nor anything false.

But he doesn't try to tell us *what* these various senses are.

Let's consider the analysis, & try to discover what senses (1) & (2) are.

(1) R. himself *suggests* (*Monist*, p. 359) "what is the sense in which one can say "There are classes", or *in other words*, what do you mean by a statement in which a class appears to come in?".

There are classes is *equivalent* to saying There are predicates coextensive with other predicates.

⟨And if you mention a particular class, e.g. "man", to say there is such a thing will mean merely that there's at least one pred. coextensive with "is a man".⟩

(2) In what sense of "There are such things as classes" will this statement be false?

This is a question which I want to discuss at some length.

[If "classes are logical] fictions" = there are no classes, & also means the same as classes are incomplete *symbols*, then it would follow that there are *no* such symbols as $\hat{z}(\phi z)$. Throughout his exposition R. seems to me to confuse in a scandalous way symbols for classes with classes, symbols for prop. functions with prop. functions, symbols for props. with props., etc.

What I want to do is to get as clear as I can (1) as to what he means by saying "So-&-so is an incomplete symbol" (2) what he means by So-&-so is a logical fiction; & then to consider in what sense, if classes are logical fictions, there are no classes.

Incomplete Symbols

R. begins by saying (*Principia*, p. 69): "By an "incomplete" symbol we mean a symbol wh. is not *supposed* to have any meaning in isolation, but is only defined in certain contexts . . . Such symbols have what may be called a "definition in use". "We define the *use* of "The author of Waverley", but "The author of Waverley" itself remains without meaning".

So p. 75: "the *uses* of symbols for classes are defined, but they themselves are not *assumed* to mean anything at all".

We can drop "not supposed to" have, & "not assumed to mean"

& we get: x is an incomplete symbol = x has no meaning in isolation = x is only defined in certain contexts = the *use* of x is defined = x *itself* has no meaning at all.

So *Monist*, p. 221. "These things, like "the author of Waverley"", wh. I call incomplete symbols, are things that have absolutely no meaning whatsoever in isolation but merely acquire a meaning in a context." "They are all incomplete symbols, i.e. they are aggregations that only have a meaning in use & do not have any meaning in themselves." (p. 222.)

Principia, p. 70. "The author of Waverley" has a meaning in use, but means nothing.

Now in all this, R. is trying to describe some difference wh. he thinks distinguishes "The author of Waverley" & "the Apostles" from *some* other symbols.

And one of the ways in wh. he tries to do this obviously, I think, fails to distinguish them from *any* other symbols. He talks as if some symbols could be defined, without its being true that their *uses* are defined. But to define a symbol is always precisely the same thing as defining its *use*.

⟨The phrase "*defined in isolation*" occurs in Ramsey's article, pp. 412 & 414[1]; where it is said (1) every incomplete symbol will be defined "not in isolation, but in conjunction with any symbol of a certain sort" (2) gives an example of a case in wh. a symbol "ϕ" can't be defined in isolation.

It seems to me, however, that he does succeed in defining ϕ in isolation

viz. $\phi =$ has either R to a or S to b.

He says $\phi x =$ xRa v xSb does *not* explain what is meant by ϕ itself, but that followed by any symbol x *it* is short for xRa v xSb; but *it* is not short for xRa v xSb; it is the whole prop. wh. is short for [it].⟩

Now what does R. mean by "has no meaning in isolation"?

What you'd think he means is: Has no meaning except when combined with other symbols into a sentence wh. expresses a prop.: but has a meaning when so combined.

But you'll notice he also says: *remains* without meaning; i.e. even when *not* in isolation: wh. looks as if he meant simply "has no meaning" whether in isolation or not; & that what he means

---

[1] [F. P. Ramsey, "Universals", *Mind*, vol. XXXIV (1925). Reprinted in F. P. Ramsey, *The Foundations of Mathematics and other Logical Essays* (London, 1931).]

is "has no meaning" but is such that a sentence in wh. it occurs has a meaning.

Moreover is there any sense in wh. "The Apostles" has a meaning in a sentence & not in isolation? If I merely utter the phrase, it certainly has in some sense some meaning, & the very same wh. it has in the sentence.

I don't want to say that there's *no* sense in wh. these symbols *have* a meaning in a sentence & *not* in isolation, but I can't find one.

And moreover there's ample reason to think that this is not *really* what R. means; that he's chosen a bad way of expressing the characteristic wh. he really means to attribute to them.

He goes on to say that the characteristic he's talking of is one wh. distinguishes such symbols from *proper names*.

And you might think, therefore, that he is holding that every symbol other than a proper name is an "incomplete symbol": this, so far as I can see, is what Ramsey means by "incomplete symbol". A precise sense *can*, I think, be given to this; but it would turn out that *all* symbols we actually use are incomplete symbols—except, perhaps, "this", as Russell himself has said. And every symbol wh. can be *analytically* defined would be an incomplete symbol.

And R. himself certainly does not mean this: he means to allow a threefold division: "incomplete symbols", proper names, symbols which are neither.

Definitions of Incomplete Symbol

x is an incomplete symbol

= (1) x *only* has a meaning *in use* (not when it is not used).

Every symbol only has a meaning in use: since to say "x has a meaning" = "x is used with a meaning".

= (2) x has a meaning, but has no meaning *in isolation*

= x is sometimes conjoined with other symbols in such a way as to form a sentence, which as a whole has a meaning, & x when so conjoined has a meaning, but except when so conjoined with other symbols, x has no meaning.

This does not appear to be true of "The author of Waverley" or "The Apostles".

= (3) Sentences in wh. x is conjoined with other symbols

have a meaning such that x helps to shew what that meaning is, but x itself has no meaning (= x has no meaning *at all*).

This is not true of "The author of Waverley" or "The Apostles".

What is meant by x "*has a meaning*"? These symbols certainly *have* got a meaning in some sense. All incomplete symbols have.

= (4) x is not a proper name.

Here we need a def. of proper name; but I think it is clear R. uses "incomplete symbol" in such a way that some symbols are *neither* proper names, nor incomplete.

= (5) x itself *can't be defined*; though sentences in which it occurs & which are such that the presence of x in them helps to convey their meaning, can be defined.

This is implied by R.'s *Principia*, 71, "we must not attempt to define x, but must define the props. in whose symbolic expression it occurs".

This, like (4), does, I think, really suggest a property which belongs to all the symbols wh. R. calls incomplete symbols; though it does not belong *only* to them, since it also belongs to proper names—in R.'s peculiar sense. And it isn't exactly right; for what is true is something I'll express by " "incomplete symbols" can only be defined by other incomplete symbols".

Possibly, by combining (4) & (5) so as to get

x is an incomplete symbol = x has meaning, but is not a proper name, & can't be *defined*

we get something wh. is both true of all the symbols wh. R. calls incomplete, & *only* of those; but of this latter I'm not sure.

But this is only true if we use *defined* in a special sense: in a sense "the author of Waverley" can be defined, & so can "the Apostles": R.'s equations *do* define these expressions.

And I don't think we can understand the sense in wh. they can't be *defined*, without going into the meaning of "definition"— wh. is in a most frightful muddle.

I've used the phrase "analytically defined"; & what I think is true is that incomplete symbols can't be "analytically defined" except by other incomplete symbols: but I've got to explain what I mean by "analytically defined"—*of a symbol*, i.e. *a word, a phrase, a sentence, a symbol*.

⟨Undoubtedly it *is* used of symbols; though there are others who say you can *also* define a notion, a property, a relation, a prop.⟩

I'll refer to an example I've given:

x is brother of y = def. x is male, & there's some animal or other of which it's true that it's a parent of x & also a parent of y. This statement of mine is an example of an analytic def. What is it that I have stated?

In asserting this I am giving an analytical def. (right or wrong) of any prop. of the form "x is brother of y".

But what am I doing? There's one thing quite certain:

I'm using 2 expressions & am asserting *either* that one *means the same as* (or means what is meant by) the other *or* am asserting that the first means so-&-so (wh. I use the second to express).

I.e. I define analytically a particular expression x, only when (1) I use another y, & either assert with regard to this other expression y that it means the same as x or assert that it means this (which I use the second to express).

But this is obviously not sufficient: for if I were to say of
x is male, etc.
this means the same as "x is brother of y"; or should say it means this, I shouldn't be defining it, either rightly or wrongly.

I am defining the expression x, only when the expression y is such that, if it does really mean the same as x (i.e. if my def. is true), then x is *short* for it. Call the 2 expressions definiendum & definiens; the definiendum must be *short for* the definiens.

But what is meant by saying that one sentence is *short* for another?

I think it's clear enough; but the sort of thing is that x is short for y if & only if (1) they both mean the same & (2) y contains more symbols which have a separate meaning than x does, so that if y does mean the same as x, there are more constituents of the prop. meant wh. have a *corresponding* symbol in y, than there are in x. (Perhaps this needs further explanation.)

Is this enough? I think so. People do say that it's also necessary that the definiens should be *understood*: but I don't think that can be necessary: certainly not that *you* should. It is necess. that the definiens shd. *have* a meaning; even if the def. is wrong.

We say then:

S is giving an analytic def. of *the expression* x = There's some *other* expression y such that (1) S is using it, (2) S either is asserting

with regard to it that it does mean the same as (means what is
meant by) x or is using it to express something of wh. he is asserting that x means that, & (3) is such that, if it does mean the same
as x, x is short for it, not *it* for x.

One very important part of what R. means by x is an incomplete
symbol is: x *in this usage* is an incomplete symbol
 [which] *entails*
In the case of *every* sentence, p, in wh. x occurs *with this meaning*,
there can be formed another sentence, q, for which p is *short* &
which is such that neither x itself nor any expression for which x
is short occurs in q.

But I said I didn't think this was *all* R. means; & I took his
statement about classes (*Principia*, 75), which implies that if a
given incomplete symbol is the sort of incomplete symbol which
"represents a class", then it can only be an incomplete symbol if it
"could be supposed to represent a class", as indicating that part
of the meaning of "x is an incomplete symbol" is "x *could be
supposed* to have such & such a property" = "looks as if it were
. . . ". *What* property exactly it must look to have I left for further
consideration.

What this extra thing is I'm now going to try to state.

Namely: in the case of every sentence in which x occurs with
this meaning, x *looks as if* it expressed an *argument* to a propl.
function expressed by the rest of the sentence, whereas in fact
it does not.

In other words: in the case of every sentence in wh. x occurs
with this meaning, the whole sentence looks as if the proposition
wh. it expressed were a value of some propl. function expressed
by the rest of the sentence whereas in fact it is not.

Thus in "The author of Waverley is Scotch", "is Scotch"
does express a function; but the prop. expressed is *not* a value
of this function, although the whole sentence looks as if it
were.

In "The author of Waverley exists", "exists" does not express
a function; but it looks as if it did, & the whole sentence looks as
if it expressed a value of this function.

If these sentences be *defined*, the definiens makes it quite plain
that this is so.

"There's some one or other who both alone wrote Waverley &

was Scotch" is obviously not a value of "x̂ was Scotch".

I think this can be put otherwise, by saying that a *value* of the prop. function "x̂ is Scotch" is a prop. such that, in asserting that prop., you are *predicating* "*is Scotch*" of something; whereas in asserting "There's something wh. both alone wrote Waverley & was Scotch", you are obviously *not* predicating "was Scotch" of anything but are predicating something of "was Scotch"; viz. that there's something wh. both had that predicate & also had another.

There remains the question how it can be that if

"The author of Waverley was Scotch"

means the same as

"There's something or other which both alone wrote Waverley & was Scotch"

& "was Scotch" means the same in both sentences, it can possibly be that "the author of Waverley" does not mean the same as [the rest of the second sentence].

All that I can say about this is that when a sentence expresses a prop., it is the fact that the symbols are conjoined in a certain way that expresses it, & that "The author of Waverley" is conjoined with "was Scotch" in a different way from that in wh. the other expression is.

My def. of how R. uses "x in this usage is an incomplete symbol" is then:

In the case of *every* sentence, p, in wh. x occurs *with this meaning*, there can be formed another sentence, q, for wh. p is short, such that neither x itself nor any expression for wh. x is short occurs in q, *and* p always *looks as if* the rest of it expressed a propl. function, such that the prop. expressed by p is a value of that function, whereas in fact it never does.

⟨You get 2 varieties, the second illustrated by E ! (ɿx)(φx); the def. of this being, you can give an analytic def. of a sentence in wh. it occurs, such that neither the expression itself nor any expression having the same meaning occurs in the definiens, & such also that the same is true of the rest of the sentence.

This is *not* true of proper names: what's true of them is that they can't be short for anything.

I don't think, however, this is *all* that R. *means* by incomplete

I

symbol: & I don't think it's a character wh. belongs *only* to what he would call incomplete symbols.

E.g. in Fairies don't exist $= \sim (\exists x) . x$ is a fairy, I think "exist" is an incomplete symbol in the sense just defined but I don't think it has the particular character wh. R. means to attribute to these. Also "fairies" is an incomplete symbol.⟩

⟨I think perh. my point about the difference in the way in which "The author of W." is used in "exists" and "is Scotch" may be made clearer by reference to the 2 generalized expressions which R. uses in *Principia* (p. 66, 30–31).

He gives

$$E ! (\imath x)(\phi x) = (\exists c) : \phi c : x \neq c . \supset_x . \sim \phi x$$
$$f(\imath x)(\phi x) = (\exists c) : \phi c : x \neq c . \supset_x . \sim \phi x : fc$$

Both of these expressions represent purely *formal* propl. functions, since ϕ and f are variables: the propl. functions in question have no *material* constituents at all.

If you substitute "wrote Waverley" for ϕ in (1) you get the prop. "the author of W. exists".

If you do the same in (2) you don't get a *prop.* at all, only a propl. function: in order to get a prop. you have *also* to substitute for f, e.g. "was Scotch" or "was a poet".

Now what's perfectly clear is that $E !$ is not a particular value of f: if it were

$$E ! (\imath x)(\phi x) \quad \text{would} \quad \text{be} = (\exists c) : \phi c : x \neq c . \supset_x . \sim \phi x : E ! c$$

which according to R. is nonsense.

But that being so surely the use of $(\imath x)(\phi x)$ in (1) *must* be different from its use in (2)? In (2) f appears on *both* sides of the equation; in $E !$ only on one: so that $E !$ has just the kind of characteristic which makes R. declare $(\imath x)(\phi x)$ to be an incomplete symbol, whereas f has not.

It seems to me this really gives us 2 different senses of "incomplete symbol", wh. it's important to distinguish.⟩

⟨A symbol, S, when used with a particular meaning, can't be defined in isolation, if either (1) Taking any expression p, expressing a prop., in which S is used with the meaning in question, then it's *logically* possible to find another expression q, expressing the same prop., and analytically defining p, such that no expression in q has the same meaning as S, and such also that

no expression in q has the same meaning as what is left of p
when S is exchanged for another constant.

This is the case of "There never was such a person as *the
author of W.*"

or (2) Taking any expression p, expressing a prop., in which S
is used with the meaning in question, it's logically possible to
find another expression q, expressing the same prop., and analytically defining p, such that *either* there's no expression in q having
same meaning as S, though there is one having same meaning as
what's left of p when S is exchanged for another constant, *or*
if there is, the expression in q which has the same meaning as S
is *not* grammatical subject of q, whereas S *is* grammatical subject
of p: = there's no expression in q wh. *both* has same meaning
as S *&* is grammatical subject of q.

This is case of "The a. of W. was Scotch".⟩

Logical Fictions

We've seen R. says that x is a logical fiction = x is an incomplete
symbol; but this is absurd.

What he means is something like: The author of Waverley is
a logical fiction = "The author of Waverley" is an incomplete
symbol.

But this won't do exactly; & I think he's wholly wrong in
supposing that there's any way in wh. he uses logical fiction,
such that from the mere fact that you've got a sentence containing
a description, you are entitled to assert the sentence obtained by
adding "is a logical fiction" to the description.

If it were so we should have to say "The large red s.d. I saw
just now is a logical fiction".

In fact the relation of the kind of incomplete symbol wh.
represents a class to "logical fiction" is quite different from that
of descriptions.

Classes are "logical fictions or constructions" =(a) symbols
for classes are incomplete symbols, (b) are not descriptions &
(c) are "logical" = every prop. or fact in the expression of which
a symbol for a class occurs, is *logically derived* from some other
prop., in the sense that it has no additional *material* constituents,
only formal ones.

⟨So "material objects are logical fictions" = symbols for

material objects (a) are incomplete symbols (b) are not descriptions.⟩

There are classes

I come now to the question of distinguishing the 2 senses of
"There are classes", viz.

(1) The sense in which, as R. says in the *Monist*, the prop.
"There are classes" is certainly true, even if R.'s definition of
sentences in wh. symbols for classes occur is correct,

& (2) the sense in wh., as he most often says, the prop. "There
are classes" is false, if R.'s def. is correct.

And I think the most important point to notice about this is
that (1) is a sense in wh. the prop. "There are classes" is *not* a
prop. about expressions; whereas (2) is a sense of "There are
classes" in wh. this *is* a prop. about symbols.

And this is one main point wh. distinguishes "logical fictions"
from *fictions*. "Logical fictions" are *not* fictions at all, whereas I
think R. supposes they are, & he uses language as if they were.
The difference is that in the case of *fictions*, e.g. fairies, or dino-
saurs, or unicorns, the prop. "unicorns are fictitious" implies
"There are no unicorns" in a sense in wh. this is *not* a prop.
about words; whereas "lions are logical fictions" only entails
"There are no lions" in a sense in wh. this *is* a prop. about words.

(1) There quite certainly *are* classes, whether R.'s view that
they are logical fictions be right or wrong.

But what is the sense in wh. there are?

"There are classes" is, it seems to me, something wh. is *logically
equivalent* to saying that there are more than one prop. of a
certain sort that are true: viz. "My fingers are a class", "The
hairs of my head are a class". *If* there are classes, at least 2 different
props. of this sort must be true; & if *one* prop. of this sort is true,
then there is at least one class. In the same way, There are men,
or There are lions, is logically equivalent to: At least 2 different
props. of the sort "This is a man" or "This is a lion" are true.
I would suggest this as a general explanation of what we mean
by "There are . . .". E.g. There are relations = at least 2 props.
of the form "Bigger than is a relation", "Near to is a relation" are
true. There are qualities = At least 2 different props. of the form
"red is a quality", "blue is a quality" are true.

In this sense it's quite clear verbally that R.'s view does not imply there are no classes. He maintains that many props. of the form "My fingers are a class" *are* true: e.g. he maintains 2 is a class, 3 is a class, & so on. The only peculiarity in his view, is in his view as to the *analysis* of such props.

This gives something *equivalent* to "There are classes"; but does it give what this *means*?

It seems to me we shall have to say what it *means* will be something different, according to the view we take as to the analysis of such props.: on R.'s view, I think it is *equivalent* to: There are at least 2 preds. or propl. functions, not coextensive with one another, with each of wh. some other predicative pred. is coextensive. If this is true, then there are more than one class; if not, not.

⟨There's no ambiguity in "There are", but only in "classes". On the ordinary view as to their analysis, we shall be asserting with regard to a certain relation expressed by "determined by" that there are things wh. have that relation to preds.⟩

I ought, perhaps, to notice that R.'s def. gives a curious result, as applied to $\hat{z}(\phi z)$ is a class.

If this is an example of $f\{\hat{z}(\phi z)\}$ then it $= (\exists \chi) : \chi \, ! \, x \, . \equiv_x . \, \phi x :$ $\{\chi \, ! \, \hat{z}\}$ is a class.

$\chi \, ! \, \hat{z}$ is a class would then need interpretation; & I suppose the interpretation must be: there's some predic. pred. coextensive with $\chi \, ! \, \hat{z}$. But I must confess I don't understand this, & may be wrong.

I've said that "there are classes" follows from any 2 different props. of the form: This is a class, That is a class.

And you might think similarly that (1) "There are imaginary beings" will follow from "Ariel is an imaginary being" & "Oberon is an imaginary being"; & that (2) "There are fairies" will follow from "Oberon is a fairy" & "Titania is a fairy". The answer to this is that though these expressions are similar, the props. expressed are not.

With regard to (1) I think the true account is to say that there is a sense in wh. it is true & a sense in wh. it's false.

(a) It's true if it means: There are sets of preds. with regard to wh. people have imagined that they all belonged to something or other, without attributing them to any real person.

(b) It's false, because self-contradictory, if it means: There are sets of preds. which both belong to something & also belong to nothing.

As for (2) I think you have simply to say that it's false, & does *not* follow from Oberon is a fairy; because this is short for "The attribute of being a fairy is one of the attributes wh. *have been attributed* to Oberon".

You *could*, if you like, say that "There are fairies" is true & means: The attribute of being a fairy has been attributed to particular imaginary characters.

But I'm not comfortable about this: one ought to be able to give a general description of the sort of props. expressible in the form "So-&-so is a ϕ" from which it will follow that there are ϕ's: and this I can't do.

"There are no classes."

This is a prop. about symbols.

And what it asserts is I think precisely the same as what I gave as meant by classes are logical fictions i.e. symbols for classes *are* incomplete & are *not* descriptions.

Thus the assertion that there are no classes amounts to saying that "determined by" in this usage does not express any relation; i.e. that "determined by" is an incomplete symbol.

One has to consider: What is the view wh. R. is opposing? What is in fact the natural view to take about props. in wh. symbols for classes occur?

The natural view is to say that there are 2 sorts of such props.:

(1) These dots are 3

(2) The pennies in my pocket, The fingers on my right hand, are 5 in number

and that in (1) "these dots" is not an incomplete symbol; in (2) "The fingers" *is* a description: namely: the entity determined by the pred. "is a finger on my right hand"; i.e. every symbol for a class is either *not* an incomplete symbol *or* if it is, *is* a description.

Thus we can say, I think, that what R. means by "there are no classes", where he says "if my def. of sentences containing class-symbols is correct, there are no classes", is *equivalent* to saying "determined by" in the usage in wh. we talk about the class "determined by" such & such a pred. is an incomplete symbol. That there are no classes in this sense, will be true if & only if "determined by" is an incomplete symbol.

Now I come to the question: Is R.'s definition of sentences containing class-symbols correct?

And this is a question which requires us to call attention to a new ambiguity in the meaning of "There are classes"; because there's a corresponding ambiguity in the meaning of "class-symbols".

R. is, in fact, using the term "class", in a sense wh., when you realise it, will seem I think to be a very queer one; viz. a sense such that *every* pred. *determines* a class; i.e. he's using "is a class" in such a sense that "ϕ is a pred. or one-valued propl. function" entails "There's one class, & one only, determined by ϕ". And this, equally, whether the pred. in question is one which is truly predicable of nothing, or of one thing only, or of more than one.

Thus he is so using "is a class", that there certainly is a class determined by "is a fairy", even if there are no fairies: it will be a class which has no members: & there's only one class wh. has no members, namely what he calls "the null-class", & the class determined by "is a fairy", if there is one, will be the same class as that determined by "is a unicorn", "is a dragon", "is a griffin", "is a hippopotamus in this room", etc.

⟨This being implied by a property wh. is certainly common to all senses of class; viz. that any 2 coextensive preds. determine the same class.⟩

Moreover he's so using it that in the case of every pred. wh. applies only to one thing, e.g. "wrote Waverley", or "is a coat wh. I am wearing", there is a class determined by each such pred.; i.e. so that there really are ever so many classes wh. have only one member each—what he calls unit-classes; & so also that a unit-class can't possibly be identical with its only member: this being a thing wh. follows from the fact that e.g. if you take the pred. "eleven wh. won the county championship this year", that is a pred. wh. belongs to only one thing, namely the Yorkshire eleven; but this thing is itself a class, wh. has eleven members, so that if you said that the unit-class "eleven wh. won the county championship" was identical with the Yorkshire eleven, you would have to say that one & the same class had both only one member & also eleven members, wh. is impossible. In other words, a pred. wh. determines a class can never be a pred. of that class; & a pred. wh. is a pred. of a class can never determine that class; & hence a unit-class can't possibly be identical with its only member—it is something *determined* by a pred. wh. is truly predicable of that member, & such therefore that that pred. can't be truly predicable of it. Thus Scott is *not* the unit-class determined by "wrote Waverley", but is its only member: a point wh. serves to bring out the distinction between descriptions & class-symbols.

In ordinary language (apart from logical works) "class" is clearly used in a very different sense; i.e. a sense such that nothing is a class but what is also "a manifold", "an aggregate" (R. says, *Principia*, 24, that he's so using "class"), "a group", "a set", "a collection": i.e. such that "ϕ is a pred." does *not* entail "There's one class & one only determined by ϕ"; but that this is only entailed by "ϕ is a pred. wh. is truly predicable of more than one thing": & such that "so-&-so is a class" entails "so-&-so is determined by a pred. wh. is truly predicable of more than one thing" = so-&-so has more than one member. I.e. the ordinary meaning of "class" is such that, by def., there can't be any null-class, or any unit-classes.

We find, then, that in order to discuss whether R.'s theory of classes is true we have to raise 2 separate questions, viz.
(1) Is it true of classes in the sense in wh. he uses it, i.e. a sense such that there certainly is a null-class & many unit-classes?

& (2) Is it true of classes in the ordinary sense, a sense such that it's logically impossible there should be a null-class or any unit-classes?

And so far as I can see, hardly anybody would be disposed to question that it is true of "classes" in the sense in wh. he uses it. If it were not, we should have to say that "determined by" expresses an *ultimate* relation, such that there really is one entity, the null-class, determined by the pred. "is a hippopotamus now in this room"; & one entity, distinct from Scott, determined by the pred. "wrote Waverley". It seems to me quite clear that there's no reason to believe in any such things; & that hence there's no reason to believe that "there are classes" with this sense of "classes" means any more than there are preds. coextensive with preds. It's obvious that "fairy" is coextensive with "unicorn", & "wrote Marmion" with "wrote Waverley".

When people think R.'s theory of classes paradoxical, it's only bec. they think it's paradoxical as applied to "classes" in the ordinary sense: R., of course, does think it applies to these also:

i.e. his view is that "class" in the ordinary sense = "class (in his sense) that has more than one member".

What reasons are there for thinking that he's wrong as to this? i.e. that the phrase "the class determined by ϕ" *is* a description?

Only that it does seem here as if "determined by" is *not* an incomplete symbol. I.e. it looks as if "having for a member" expresses an ultimate relation, different from "characterising", & such that nothing can have *one* member without having more than one.

I know of no argument against the view that "determined by" as applied to classes with several members is *not* an incomplete symbol: the only arg. mentioned by Whitehead & Russell, viz. that if so there would be something wh. really is both one & many, does *not* seem to me a strong one.

Is "There are many" incompatible with "There are one"?

There's hardly any word used in philosophy so ambiguous as "unity", & it's quite certain that there are many senses of "one" such that "There are many" is not incompatible with "There are one" = form a unity.

The only question, then, can be as to whether "There are many" is incompatible with there are *one* in *the* sense in wh. the view that "is a member of" expresses a relation not identical with "characterised by", involves that what has members is one.

What *is* this sense?

It seems to me that the sense is only this: viz. that there's some pred. or other such that anything wh. has members is *only* one (= not many) of the things wh. have that pred.

But this isn't immediately evident: let me explain how I get at it.

What senses of "one" are there in wh. "one" is incompatible with many?

Only those senses in which is *one* entails this is *only* one (*not many*).

(1) And there are such senses: "This is one man" does entail "This is *only* one man"; "This is one of these" does entail "This is *only* one of these".

I.e. there are predicates such that "This (or these) is *one* of the things wh. have this pred." does entail "This or these is *only* one (not many) of the things wh. have it".

⟨And this is in fact how we commonly use the word, i.e. relatively to a specific pred.⟩

But these are senses in which you can only talk of "only one" or "one" relatively to a *given* pred. What you are saying is: This is *one* relatively to this pred.; wh. is incompatible with: This is many relatively to this.

(2) If you want to get a sense in wh. you can use "one" & "only one" *absolutely*, you have to take a sense derived from this, in the way in wh. absolute preds. are derived from relative.

This is *one* relatively to some predicate

= There's *some* pred. such that this is only *one* of the things that have it.

This gives: one relatively to some pred., & only *one* relatively to some pred.

And there's no obvious reason why this shouldn't be compatible with: There's *some* predicate (another one) such that this is *many* of the things wh. have it.

Certainly in the case of every class there is a pred. such that the class in question is only one of the things wh. have it: e.g. the pred. of being a class of this order; & there's also some such that it's many relative to that pred., viz. any pred. wh. determines the class.

There seems to me, therefore, to be nothing in the objection that nothing can be both one & many.

It seems to me a much more serious objection that we seem to have to admit in the case of classes that there are certain classes wh. are both *one* relatively to a certain pred. & also *many* relatively to the *same* pred.

This would really be impossible, if "one relatively to this pred." always entailed *only* one relatively to this pred.; as it might well seem to do.

And every class of classes really is both one class & also many classes: e.g. The First class county elevens are a class, & are also many classes.

But I think all we have to say is that there are certain preds. such that x can be *one* of the things that have that pred. & also *many*: i.e. that it's not true of *all* preds. that x is *one* of the things that have this pred. entails x is *only* one of the things wh. have it.

This is *not* a case of a sense of one, such that is one is incompatible with is many.

II

NECESSITY

(1) "There is such a thing as this sense-datum" expresses a fact.

(2) The fact which it expresses is one of which the contradictory is self-contradictory & yet the fact in question is not a necessary fact.

(3) It is *not* necessary, because "There *might* have been no such thing as this sense-datum" also expresses a fact. ⟨I'm not quite sure of this.⟩

(4) "There might have been . . ." is *not* equivalent to " "There *is* no such thing as this sense-datum" *might* have been true": "There is no such thing as this sense-datum" *couldn't* have been true, because it is self-contradictory. What it *is* equivalent to is: "There *might have been* no such prop. as "There is such a thing as this sense-datum" nor yet as "There is no such thing as this sense-datum" ". ⟨Call this: p *subsists* contingently.⟩

(5) It's *not* the case, therefore, that wherever ∼ p entails a contradiction, p is a necessary truth: it's *only* the case that where *both* ∼ p entails a contradiction & p subsists necessarily, *then* p is necessary.

Hence there are 2 different kinds of contingent truth.

(6) It's therefore also *not* the case that p entails q only where p ⊃ q is a necessary truth. For, p ⊃ q can be a necessary truth only where "There might have been no such prop. as p ⊃ q" is false; and there might have been no such prop. as p ⊃ q wherever there might have been no such prop. as p or as q; & there certainly might have been no such prop. as "This sense-datum is round & white", & therefore none such as "This sense-datum is round & white" ⊃ "This sense-datum is white".

If we make this distinction between props. wh. subsist contingently & props. wh. subsist necessarily, then with regard to any pair of props., p & q, obviously there are the following four alternatives open, viz.

(1) p & q may both subsist necessarily

(2) p & q may both subsist contingently

(3) p may subsist necessarily & q contingently

(4) p may subsist contingently & q necessarily.

129

And I have to say with regard to the sense in wh. I use "entails", that so far as I can see, in cases (1), (2) & (4) it is possible that p may entail q, but in (3) it is impossible that p should entail q.

Examples of entailing in (1), (2) & (4).

(1) There are red things *entails* There are coloured things.

(2) This is red *entails* This is coloured.

(4) This is red *entails* There is at least one red thing.

But now take a case of (3), where it is often supposed that q follows from p.

p = "Whatever is red is coloured"

q = "This is red ⊃ This is coloured".

I say that p does *not* entail q; but only p together with "There is such a prop. as "This is red" ".

And my reason is that I want to say p entails q *only* where it's inconceivable that p should be true & q *not* true; only where in any possible universe in wh. p was true, q would be true too.

Now here it certainly is inconceivable that p should be true & q false; but not at all inconceivable that p should be true & q *not* true, since it's not inconceivable that p should be true, & that there should be no such prop. as q.

It doesn't matter whether you use "entails" to cover this case or not; but what *does* matter, if I'm right, [is] that you should not overlook the difference between

It's inconceivable that p should be true & q *not* &

It's inconceivable that p should be true & q *false*.

(2) may be true where (1) is false; so we ought to distinguish between a relation wh. holds *only where* (1) is true, & one that holds also in cases where (1) is not true.

What seems to me to be true is:

Every prop. in wh. a *particular* is a constituent subsists contingently.

Every prop. in wh. *no* particular is a constituent subsists necessarily.

We can say P is a predicate wh. subsists contingently when & only when the prop. (∃x) . Px subsists contingently

& P is a pedicate wh. subsists necessarily when & only when the prop. (∃x) . Px subsists necessarily.

And, if so, then every pred. in wh. a particular is a constituent will subsist contingently.

And every pred. in wh. *no* particular is a constituent subsists necessarily.

Thus in my view every *purely abstract* pred. subsists necessarily but *all* preds. that are *not* purely abstract subsist only contingently.
⟨p subsists contingently = There might have been no such prop. as p
= In some possible Universe there would have been no such prop. as p
= p might have been neither true nor false.
This last seems at first sight to be inconsistent with the Law of Excluded Middle.

But it is *not* inconsistent with

Every actual prop. *is* either true or false

nor with

Every actual prop. *must* be either true or false if this means:
If p *had* been false, ∼ p would have been true.

It's only inconsistent with

If p had *not* been true, ∼ p would have been true.⟩

III

PROPOSITIONS AND TRUTH

The next epistemol. questions wh. I propose to consider are 2 questions wh. are often confused with one another: viz. (1) What is Truth? & (2) What (if any) is the criterion or test of truth?

You might at first sight think that neither of these are epistemolog. questions at all: neither of them, at first sight, seem to be questions about *knowledge*, nor even about cognition. Yet it seems to me quite certain that the word epistemology is ordinarily used in such a way that both are so. And as regards the second I think the explanation is simple: viz. that the question *is* really a question about knowledge: what is meant is: what criterion is there by which we can *know* whether a given prop. is true or false? As regards the first, I really don't know *why* it is called epistemological: the best reason I can suggest is that it's a question an answer to which must be included in any complete answer to the question as to what is the nature of 2 species of cognition—viz. belief & conceiving the hypothesis that: each of these is such that *what* is believed or conceived *must* be either true or false; & you couldn't give a complete account of their nature without explaining *why* this is so; nor this without explaining what truth is. But I will confess that the reason why I'm treating it now is bec. (2) is a question about knowledge wh. I want to treat; & I don't think it can be treated as clearly as it should be without also treating (1), which, as I say, is apt to be confused with it.

What is Truth?

You are prob. familiar with 3 names which are sometimes supposed to be names of 3 radically different answers to this question—each of wh. has many living adherents: viz. "The correspondence theory of truth", "The coherence theory of truth" & "The pragmatist or pragmatic theory of truth". People who use the names don't, I think, in general know at all clearly what they mean by them; & I've no doubt they are often used in different senses by different people. In particular with regard to the last 2, what is often meant is a theory as to the *criterion* of truth, *not* as to what truth is.

What I'm going to say is that the 2 last are quite certainly false in all their forms; & that *a* correspondence theory of truth is certainly the right answer to our question. This is not to say that *many* forms of correspondence theory are not false: there's no such thing as *the* correspondence theory. My main object will be to try to define *which* correspondence theory is the true one.

The word "true" is used in several different senses: & before we proceed to discuss *what* it means, it's essential to try to point out *which* of the senses in wh. it is used is the one we're dealing with.

The sense or senses I'm concerned with may, I think, be described by saying it is the one (or all the ones) in which many *propositions* are true, & in which nothing but *props.* are true. And we shall, of course, also be concerned with a corresponding sense or senses of "false", namely one in wh. many props. are false, & in which nothing *but* a prop. is false.

And, I think, this is *perhaps* sufficient to *describe* it; but I'm not *quite* certain, since I think it's possible that the term "proposition" is used ambiguously, & that the sense in wh. a prop. can be true, in one of its senses, is different from that in wh. it can be true in another. I think it's almost certain that many *philosophers* use prop. in a sense different from that in wh. it's ordinarily used; philosophers having a great tendency to use words out of their proper senses, because they take a false view as to the analysis of the ordinary sense (as with physical objects), & then occasionally at least use the word with the connotation they imagine to be the ordinary one: most other uses of prop. seem to me to arise from a false analysis of the true one.

There is *a* sense of prop. such that whenever anybody believes *that* so-&-so or conceives the hypothesis that so-&-so, he can be truly said to be believing the *proposition* that so-&-so or conceiving the *proposition* that so-&-so.

I.e. S is believing that it will be dark soon entails S is believing *the prop.* that it will be dark soon; S is conceiving the hypothesis that Ariel was imprisoned in a tree by the witch Sycorax entails S is conceiving *the prop.* that.

This gives a vague descr. of one (or several) uses of prop.; but it does not profess to give any analytic def. of p is a proposition; & it leaves open the question whether propositions are single entities, or, as R. at one time believed, are logical constructions— i.e. that S believes that it will be dark soon does *not* assert of any dual relation that S has that relation to a single entity, but only that he has a multiple relation to several different entities.

What it does is to connect the meaning of "*prop.*" in a definite manner with something which we all are familiar with, i.e. what is meant by believing *that* so-&-so or conceiving *that* so-&-so: but it doesn't say anything as to the *analysis* of this pred.

The question *what* a prop. is, in this sense, can only be answered by an analysis of this kind of expression & I don't think anyone knows what the analysis is.

Many philosophers have said things wh. imply that prop. can be used in other senses; but it may be doubted whether they actually use them in others. They adopt a false view as to 2 such senses.

E.g. Keynes says, p. 66.[1]

(1) "A judgment expressed *in language* is precisely what is meant by a prop.".

Now, even if we suppose that he means by "a judgment" something wh. has been judged by somebody & not an act of judgment, this sense of prop. is clearly a different one from ours.

For it excludes

(a) props. wh. have been conceived, but never believed ⟨judged⟩

(b) props. which have been believed, but never *expressed* at all

(c) props. which have been both believed & expressed, but expressed not in language but e.g. in symbols.

I doubt myself whether there's *any* sense of prop., in wh. a prop. means what Keynes says; but he's certainly wrong in saying this is the *only* sense.

(2) He immed. goes on to say something apparently inconsistent with what he's just said: viz. "So far as we treat of propositions in logic, we treat of them not as grammatical sentences, but as assertions, as verbal expressions of judgments".

Now Logic certainly professes to deal with *all* props.; & hence Keynes implies that *all* props. are verbal expressions of judgments; though not necessarily that all verbal expressions of judgments are props.

This is obviously inconsistent with what he has just said, unless it is true, as at first sight seems very unlikely, that every judgment is itself both (a) a verbal expression & also (b) a verbal expression *of* another verbal expression.

[1] [J. N. Keynes, *Formal Logic*, 4th edition (London, 1906).]

And also it is something which can't be true of *our* sense of prop., unless whenever anybody believes or conceives *that* so-&-so, both (1) that so-&-so *is* a verbal expression; i.e. we could say S believes *the verbal expression* that the sun is larger than the moon & (2) whenever anybody *conceives* that so-&-so, we can say not only: he conceives *the* verbal expression that Ariel was imprisoned in a tree by the witch Sycorax, but also this verbal expression is a verbal expression of a judgment.

But this is a view which implies the prop.:

All props. are *expressions*

and this view, in general, is one wh. is very commonly taken.

I pointed out that many philosophers have certainly supposed there is a sense in which "proposition" may be properly used, wh. is such that *every* proposition is also an expression.

But I should have said also that most philosophers who suppose this, suppose also that there is a sense of "prop." such that "p is a prop." *entails* "p is an expression"; and I think if we admit the former we must admit this too: for it's difficult to see how we could possibly know the former, unless we know this.

Keynes, e.g., obviously means to say "p is a prop." = def. "p is a verbal expression of a judgment"; &, if so, then obviously p is a prop. *entails* p is an expression, since p is a verbal expression etc. entails this.

I then went on to consider whether the sense of prop. that *I* have described is a sense of wh. this is true. *If* mine is a proper sense at all, philosophers have certainly frequently implied this, since they have implied that the *only* sense of prop. is one of wh. this is true.

And I said *this* is certainly false: i.e. there *is* a sense of prop. such that it's not true that "is a prop." entails "is an expression" or that every prop. is an expression.

If it were true, then whenever we can truly say "S is believing that the sun is larger than the moon", or "S is believing that it will be dark soon", we should also be able to say truly "S is believing the expression that the sun is larger than the moon", "S is believing the expression that it will be dark soon"; since my sense of prop. is such that "S is believing p" entails "S is believing the prop. p"; &, if every prop. *is* an expression, it would follow that whenever the one is true the other is.

K

I think this is one of the clearest ways of bringing out the falsity of the view that we *always* use prop. in such a sense that every prop. is an expression.

But now, I said I wanted to go on to consider the view that *sometimes*, though not always, what is a prop., in my sense, is also an *expression*.

If this were so, it would seem to follow that *sometimes*, though not always, when it is true that S is believing p, he is also believing *the expression* p.

This view can be put in the form: *Some*, but not all, of the things wh. are props. in my sense, are also *expressions*.

Now I believe this view also is false; & to shew that it *is* false, is the nearest I can come to explaining what a prop. in my sense is.

But in order to do this, it is necessary to do what I have not yet done, that is, to raise the question what "an expression" is. This, it seems to me, is certainly itself an ambiguous expression; the ambiguity is one that's very important, but wh. it seems to me very difficult to express quite clearly.

We can give as a general def. of "expression": x is an expression = by means of x somebody has expressed something.

But this def. is itself ambiguous in the way I mean. The ambiguity in question is the one of wh. R. is talking (*Principia*, vol. I, 2nd ed., p. 664) when he talks of "the difference between propositions considered factually & props. as vehicles of truth & falsehood", & concludes "A proposition as the vehicle of truth or falsehood is a particular occurrence, while a prop. considered factually is a class of similar occurrences"; & to which C. S. Peirce referred when he said the phrase "a word" is ambiguous, & proposed to distinguish the 2 senses by saying that in the one sense every word is a *token* & not a type, in the other every word is a *type* & not a token.

I'll begin to try to explain the ambiguity by taking the instance of words. It seems to me very difficult to state *exactly* what the truth about the matter is.

I have written up *the word* "*sun*" twice upon the board. This is certainly true. But *what* is it that I've written *twice*? I've written *this* once, & *this* once, neither of them twice. But quite certainly *in a sense* of the word "word", this is one word, & that is another word: they are *not* the same word: I've written 2 words & *not* one word twice. But in another sense: this is the same word as

that; this is the word "sun" & that is the word "sun": & since
we should naturally take the "is" here to stand for identity, we
seem to be contradicting ourselves, since this is *not* identical
with that, & yet each of them *is identical* with the word "sun".
It seems to me that the sense of "word" in wh. we must admit
that there are 2 words & *not* one word is a sense we comparatively
rarely use: but we do use it, e.g. in answering the question how
many words there are in a given line of print or on a given page:
nobody would say that in "*The* sun is larger than *the* moon"
there were only 6 words, on the ground that the first *the* is the
same word as the second *the*: & yet they certainly *are* the same
word. The sense of "word" in which there are 2 different words,
is that sense of "word" in which every word is a *token* & none
is a *type*; the sense of word in wh. they are the same word is that
in which no word is a *token*, but every word is a *type*.

There are, of course, still further ambiguities wh. it's perhaps
worth while to call attention to. I'll write up "sol", "soleil",
"Sonne". Each of these is not only a different token from "sun",
but also a different *type*. But etymologically *Sonne* is the *same*
word as sun, & perhaps the others are too—I don't know.

Now the question I want to raise is the question: What is *the*
word "*sun*"? *This* is certainly not identical with it, *nor* is *that*;
& yet each of them *is* the word "sun". R. says that the word
"Socrates" is a class of series; & perhaps he would say the same
of "sun": in any case he would say that it is a *class*. But this is
certainly not quite correct. When we say: "This is the word *sun*",
we're not saying that this is a class; nor when we say "The word
sun has been written up twice" are we saying of any class that it
has been. What seems to me quite plain is that we are talking of a
certain predicate, & are saying that this & that both have that
predicate.

This pred. determines a class—what we can call if we like all
"instances *of the word* "*sun*" ". But it's not correct to say that the
word "sun"—the type—is either the predicate or the class. It's
the sort of case where it's tempting to say that there is no such
thing as the word "sun"; that the word "sun" is a fiction; that
words as types are all fictions. But even this is not I think correct.
There certainly is such a thing as the word "sun". But what is
meant by this is only: There are token-words wh. share this
predicate—that of being similar to *this* token-word, *or* related to

it in the way in wh. this noise is related to that scratch, or to those printed letters.

I think we can say this: that "the word "sun" " is always equivalent to some phrase of the form "*some* token-word having this pred." or "*any* token-word having the predicate" or "*a* token-word". Thus: *this* is the word—sun = this is a token-word having this predicate—the predicate of being related in a certain way to the token-noise I use: i.e. my prop. is *about* this noise.

What does: "This is the same word as that" mean? This token-word shares with that *a* predicate of a certain sort.

Now there is obviously just the same ambiguity about "sentence" & "expression". I have written down the *same* sentence twice over; but I have also written 2 *different sentences*. We require, therefore, to use the phrases: "token-sentence" & "token-expression".

And the def.

x is an expression = by means of x somebody has expressed something⎱is ambiguous, bec. it *may* mean "By means of this token-expression somebody has expressed something" or "By means of *some* token-expression having *this* predicate (a pred. wh. belongs to x) somebody has expressed something".

But now, if we raise question: Are any things wh. are props. in our sense also expressions?, we need to know whether this means "token-expressions" or not; & also what's meant by saying that so-&-so *is both* a prop. & *an expression*.

Now (1) there's no question whatever that no *prop.* in our sense is *identical with* any token-expression.

When I say S is believing that the sun is larger than the moon, there is *no* token-expression wh. I am either mentioning or describing, of wh. I am saying that S is believing *that*. I am indeed *uttering* a token-expression; but I'm certainly not saying that he's believing that one;

& (2) there's also no question that *no* prop. in our sense is *identical* with any type-expression.

Only here we have to consider what would be meant by saying that it is identical with one—considering what a queer sort of entity a type-expression is.

To say it was identical would be to say that "S believes the prop. the sun is larger than the moon" = def. "S is believing *some* token* wh. has the predicate wh. we assert of this when we say it *is* the sentence "the sun is larger than the moon" ". But this is certainly *not* the case. What we say is something wh. certainly may be true when he's not doing this, but e.g. using some token-sentence, wh. is of the type-sentence "Sol maior est quam luna".

The only sense in wh. it *might* be true that *some* props. in our sense *are* expressions would be this.

Namely, it might be held that in the same queer sense in wh. we can say of this token-expression that it *is* the type-expression "the sun is larger than the moon"; so we can sometimes say of a token-expression that it *is* the prop. "the sun is larger than the moon"; although the pred. wh. we assert of it when we say the one will be different from that wh. we assert when we say the other.

And the theory as to what we mean by "S is believing that the sun is larger than the moon" would be "S is believing some token-expression wh. *is* the prop. that the sun is larger than the moon"; & that this same token-expression *is* also a type-expression.

To say that a certain token-expression *is* this prop. would *not* be to say that it's identical with it, but that it possesses a certain pred.; & the pred. will *never* be the same as that wh. we assert it to have when we say it is the expression so-&-so. How it would differ can, I think, be easily seen. The group of token-expressions wh. are instances of *the prop.* the sun is larger than the moon would be a very much larger group than that of those wh. are instances of *the type-expression* the sun is larger than the moon. It would include *all* these, & also all token-expressions which are instances of expressions that have *the same meaning* as "the sun is larger than the moon": e.g. le soleil est plus grand que la lune: sol maior est quam luna; Die Sonne ist grösser als der Mond, etc.

Now in the theory there is *one* part wh. it seems to me may quite well be true & it is an important suggestion: viz. that just as in "S made use of ⟨uttered⟩ the *expression*: It will be dark soon", what we are saying is *quite certainly* of the form "S made use of *some* token having this predicate"; so in "S was believing the prop.: It will be dark soon" what we are saying is of the form "S was believing *some* token which had this pred.". In other words it suggests that the phrase "the prop." is like the phrase "the expression", in respect of the fact that there are many particular facts which can be called tokens, since they stand to it in the same relation in wh. words, in the sense in wh. these are 2 words, stand to "the word "sun" ".

⟨There is *some* relation R & *some* pred. ϕ such that what we're asserting is of the form "S had R to *some* thing wh. has the pred. ϕ". This we *might* express by saying: There are token-props.⟩

This *may* be true; I see nothing against it; though also nothing *for* it. It gives a suggestion as to the analysis of "is believing the prop. that".

The point with which I ended last time is, I think, a perfectly clear one.

I said that if you consider expressions of the form "S used *the expression* x", there is always some predicate such that what is being asserted is that S used *some* token-expression having that predicate.

E.g. suppose I *utter* with regard to a particular person S & a particular time t the words "S at the time t used the expression "Tails differ greatly in length" ".

Then in order that the prop. about S wh. I am expressing should be true, it is absolutely necessary that *either*

(1) S should at t have spoken in succession a series of sounds *very* similar to those wh. I utter in saying "Tails differ greatly in length": of course, *not* those particular sounds themselves, nor any *exactly* like them, but *very* similar

or (2) S should|at t have written down in succession a series of visible or tangible letters or other marks, of a kind such that marks of that kind have been commonly used to represent sounds of the kind mentioned in (1). Many very different kinds of marks will all do equally well: S may have used the Gk. or Hebrew alphabet; or may have used shorthand. That is *written* token-sentences need not *resemble* one another at all closely to be the *same* type-sentence; whereas *sound* token-sentences have to. What makes written token-sentences the same type-sentence is not similarity, but their having the same relation to a given sound type-sentence.

I'm not sure that *either* of these necessary conditions is *sufficient*.

(Moreover when I say this I am talking about the particular token-sounds I utter & am saying that S used at t *either* some token-sounds resembling those & having perhaps some other relation *or* some written letters or marks related to them in a certain way.)

For suppose S uttered sounds satisfying (1) but meant what we write "Tales differ greatly in length", would he have been using the same expression? I don't feel sure.

Or suppose he had written "Tales differ greatly in length", he would have satisfied (2): but would he have used the expression in question, if what I meant by the sound was "Tails differ greatly in length"? I'm not sure.

Suppose in expressions of the form: S at t was believing p, the prop. expressed is always of the following form: viz. There is a pred. ϕ & a relation R, such that what we're expressing is that S at t had R to *some* entity wh. possessed ϕ.

We can define: *There are token-propositions* to mean that this theory is true; & can say that an entity is a token-proposition if & only if somebody at some time has had to it either R or Q (the corresponding relation in the case of conceiving), & also it has had *some* pred. of the kind, which is such that x is believing a prop. *only* if he has R to an entity having some pred. of the kind.

This *may* be true; & is *part* of what R. is asserting in *Analysis of Mind*.[1]

But it's to be noted that even if it is true, there will be an important difference between the relation of token-props. to type-props., & that of token-expressions to type-expressions.

The difference is that we never *use* the name "prop." for "token-props.", whereas we *do* use "word" *both* for "token-word" & for "type-word".

⟨If you want to count the number of different *props.* asserted in a page, there won't be 2 different ways of counting, so long as you're using prop. in my sense.⟩

And in consequence of this it can't be the case that what we mean by "believe" is a name for a relation to token-props. Since I've defined "prop." in such a way that whenever you say S believes p, you can also say S believes the prop. p.

I.e. whereas S *utters* the word "sun" = *utters* some token-word having ϕ; S *believes* the prop. "Sun is larger than moon" can't = "S believes some token-prop. having χ", but *must* be S

---

[1] [B. Russell, *The Analysis of Mind* (London, 1921).]

has R to some token-prop. having χ, where R is different from "believes".

On both these points R. is suggesting a mistake: he suggests that what he calls image-props. & word-props. are props. in some sense in wh. we commonly use that word, & also that they are believed.

There is one other argument I want to use; but wh. I find it difficult to express. A prop. is true if & only if there is some fact wh. directly verifies it, & false if & only if there is some fact wh. directly negates it. And the relation of the prop. in each case to the fact is *necessary*, not accidental: that *prop. couldn't* have been verified or negated by any *other* fact than this one. Of all token-expressions, even in the wide sense, this is not true: the connection of any expression with the fact wh. verifies or negates it is accidental. I don't mean that they're all conventional; some may be natural. But it's always logically possible that that expression should have expressed something else.

Hence I think it's clear that the sense of "true" in wh. expressions are "true" is different from that in wh. props. in our sense are "true".

To say that an expression is true is simply to say that it *expresses* a true prop.

What then *does* "true" mean in our sense?

In order to answer this question, the first thing necess. is to call attention to an undoubted fact: viz. that p *either* means the same as *or* is logically equivalent to p is true.

I explained that the sense (or senses) of "true" with which I'm concerned is that (or those) in which many *props.* are true, & *only* props. are true; & I've now tried to shew that the sense of *prop.* with wh. I'm concerned is *not* a sense in which every prop. is also an expression, but on the contrary one in wh. (1) no prop. is identical with any expression & (2) even if there are token-props. no token-prop. is identical with any token-expression.

With regard to senses of prop. in which every prop. is also an expression, I admit that there is a sense in wh. such props. can be said to be true; but it seems to me obvious that every such sense is one which can only be defined in terms of our sense—to say an expression is true = it expresses a true prop.

It is primarily *token-expressions* wh. are "true" in this sense:

with regard to a *type-expression* to say that it was "true" would be to say that *every* token-expression wh. was an instance of it was true, & this is a thing which it would be rash to affirm was ever the case; since, in general, different token-expressions which are instances of the same type-expression express different props., & it would be rash to affirm of *any* type-expression that it has never been used to express a prop. wh. was false: the most we can ever affirm is, of certain type-expressions, that *if* used in their proper sense, they have always expressed true props.: e.g. 2 + 2 = 4 or "the sun is larger than the moon". It would be rash to assume that these expressions have never been used by anyone in a sense in wh. they expressed false props.

But now what is meant by "true" in that sense or those senses of the term in wh. nothing but props. in our sense are true?

There is one fundamental fact, extremely obvious but constantly overlooked, which is such that no answer to this question can be right, unless it is consistent with it. And it is because *only* a correspondence-theory as to what truth is, is consistent with it, that I say some such theory must be right; & because all coherence & pragmatist theories wh. are answers to this question are inconsistent with it, that I say they are certainly wrong.

The fact is this. For all values of p, where p is a prop. in our sense (1) p is true if & only if p; or to put it in another way; (2) in order that p should be true, it is both a necessary & sufficient condition that p; or finally (3) p is true both entails & is entailed by p.

Put in ways (1) & (2) it sounds rather queer, but if you take any particular prop., no matter what you take, it is at once obvious both what it means & that it is true.

E.g. (1) It is true that the sun is larger than the moon if & only if the sun *is* larger than the moon.

(2) In order that it should be true that the sun is larger than the moon, it is both a necessary & a sufficient condition that the sun should be larger than the moon.

It seems to me quite indisputable that in the case of every prop. without exception this is true; & hence any answer to the question what "true" means must be such that p is true will *both entail & be entailed by* p. We can start from this fact, in asking what it *does* mean; but the answer is not perfectly obvious.

The fact I've stated does in fact strongly suggest the view that *sometimes*

"p is true" *means precisely the same as* "p", & if this were *always* the case, then it seems to me the only correct answer to our question would be that "true" *means nothing at all.*

That this *is* the only correct answer would follow from Wittgenstein's principle (5. 141)[1] "If p follows from q & q from p they are one & the same proposition" (provided he is, as I think, using prop. in our sense). And Johnson seems to take the same view in I, p. 52, although so far as I can see what he there says is quite inconsistent with what he says elsewhere.

He raises the question "Is "p-is-true" a secondary prop.?" and seems to hold (1) that *in general* it isn't: "p is true" is *in general* reducible to the simple prop. p; (2) that we may say *strictly* that the adjective *"true"* is redundant as applied to p: wh. should mean "p" & "p is true" *always* mean the same; & (3) p-true is *practically indistinguishable* from p; wh. should mean *always*.

This is inconsistent with 4 things each also inconsistent with one another (1) "true" is indefinable (p. 8), wh. implies it has meaning, (2) p. xxxiv "p is true" is to be identified with "p ought to be accepted" (denied on p. 8), (3) "the truth of a judgment (expressed in a prop.) may be said to *mean* that the prop. is in accordance with a certain fact" & (4) " "matter exists" is true" means any thinker who might assert it would be exempt from error.

Now it seems to me

(1) that *sometimes* we do use "p is true" to mean exactly the same as "p": I think we *always* do so when we say "S is believing that p is true", or S is doubting whether p is true, wondering etc. (J. p. 52).

But

(2) if we always did, it would, so far as I can see, be inexplicable that we should ever talk of "truth" at all.

I said

"p is true" is *always* logically equivalent to, & is perhaps always or sometimes identical with, "if anyone were to believe p, he would, so far as he were believing *that*, be believing truly or correctly" (we saw J. on p. 3–4 said something very like this).

---

[1] [L. Wittgenstein, *Tractatus Logico–Philosophicus* (London, 1922).]

And we may, therefore, at least possibly get a hint as to what true means, by considering what *this* means.

But in order to discover what this means, we have to consider what can be meant by "S was believing p, & was so far believing correctly".

Well, it seems to me quite clear that sometimes, at least, the following is meant.

Consider what it is that any one of us *discovers* when he *discovers* that a past belief of his own as to the future was correct.

Suppose I believe at a given time "It will soon be dark".

I subsequently find or discover (= know) that it is dark, & know also that the time at which it is dark is only a little later than the time at wh. I believed it would soon be dark.

I find or discover the fact "it was going to be dark soon after *that* time" (the time of the belief).

And I can see that a certain one-one relation holds between the predicate wh. then attached to me viz. "believing that soon after t it will be dark", & the fact "soon after t it was going to be dark".

The relation in question is in fact the one owing to the existence of wh. I use the same language to express the fact as I use to express the prop. I believed. Of course, the language is not *quite* the same: the one expression is "It will be dark soon after *now*", the other "It was going to be dark soon after *then*". But if *now* I talk of my past belief, I say: I believed it was going to be dark soon after now.

I see that a certain one-one relation holds between the predicate & the fact: i.e. a relation which that pred. *couldn't* have had to more than one fact, & which no other pred. could have had to that fact.

This relation, I have to admit, is one for which, so far as I can see, we have no name in common use: philosophers often call it *corresponding*, but corresponding is too vague. I'm going to call it: is *directly* verified by. I say *directly* bec. the pred. is *indirectly* verified by its being of *this* degree of darkness; & by any other fact wh. *proves* that it's dark: i.e. by anything whatever from which the fact wh. directly verifies follows. And to be verified by a fact is thus *not* a one-one relation: the same belief may be proved to be true by each of very different facts.

But to be directly verified in my sense is a one-one relation.

And what I want to suggest is that what we mean by "in so

far as I had that pred., I was believing correctly" is simply *"that*
predicate was directly verified by *some* fact".

In the case of any particular belief we can express something
logically equivalent to this in another way: e.g. I believed that it
was going to be dark, & it *was* going to be dark. If that is true,
then the pred. must have been directly verified by *some* fact; &
if the pred. was directly verified by some fact, this must be true,
since the only fact that *could* directly verify it would be the fact
that it was going to be dark. But if we want to speak of a characteristic common to different predicates of this sort, the only one we
can take is that of being directly verified by *some* fact.

One further point, & we get an analytic def. of "true", as
applied to props.

It is quite obvious that in the case of every pred. wh. is directly
verified by *some* fact, there is another one-one relation wh. the
prop. related to the pred. in the way expressed by saying that that
pred. is that of "is believing this prop." has to *some* fact, & always
to the *same* fact. Whether or not "directly verified" as applied to
preds. is to be defined in terms of this other relation, or vice versa,
I don't pretend to say: it's only in the latter case that *is true*
could be *identical* with "anyone who believed p, would be believing
correctly". Let's call the other relation "directly proved by".

Then I say: p is true = p is directly proved by some fact.

I've here *described* what relation I mean by directly proved:
I haven't analysed it but I *have* analysed "true".

It seems to me obvious & undeniable that this is how we
originally got at the notion of "true" as applied to props.: viz.
we know in particular cases that we have believed a certain prop.;
we *find* that this pred. has been directly verified by this fact; &
we therefore say that the prop. we believed was true, meaning that
it had to *some* fact *the* one-one relation wh. it follows that it has
from the fact that the pred. was directly verified.

And this account is confirmed by considering the corresponding
account of "false".

Here what we have to start from is that in certain cases we
know we believed a certain prop., e.g. about the future, & we
then *find* a certain fact, which has a certain one-one relation to
the prop. in question. E.g. we believe that S will be in a certain
room; or that S will not be in a certain room: we open the door &
find he's *not* there, or find he is there.

In *both* cases we perceive that the prop. we believed has to that particular fact the same one-one relation—viz. one wh. I will call "is directly negated by"—a relation to wh. it is due that the contradictory of the expression wh. expresses the prop. expresses the fact.

It has sometimes been suggested that "false" = "not true": in wh. case p is false would = p is not directly proved by any fact.

But it seems to me quite plain that "false" is a positive conception; i.e. that there's a positive relation such that we're saying: has this positive relation to some fact.

It has been suggested that we form the conception "false", before we form the conception "true"; & that if we hadn't in certain cases found props. to be false, we should never have found the conception "true" at all. I think this is very prob. true. But the relation "being directly proved by" is certainly one wh. could *theoretically* have been noticed, without our ever having noticed the relation "is directly negated by", i.e. it is *not* definable in terms of it.

I define *a* coherence-theory of truth (in our sense) to be one which says

There is some *many-membered class* such that p is true *includes* the prop. "p is coherent with many members of this class".

And by "coherence" is meant *not* mere consistency; *nor* yet entailing; "p is coherent with q" *includes* the assertion "q confirms p" or "renders p probable", in the 2 senses appropriate acc. as q is a fact or a prop.

It's *not* a theory wh. says "coherent with *some* thing".

Many different coherence theories can be held acc. as different views are taken as to *what* the class is, & as to *what* p is true asserts *besides* that p is coherent with many members of it.

E.g. the class wh. *I* refer to by "p is true" may be held to mean "*my* experience" = all the props. I believe & facts I know.

And it may be held (1) that p is true = p is coherent with a majority of these, wh. would give more true or less true acc. as a greater or less majority

(2) that p is true = p is coherent with many, wh. wd. give more or less true acc. as more or less.

It has to be remembered that the view is one wh. really arises from confusion with *coherence* as a *test* of truth; & that what people are here thinking of is being confirmed by a large number of other facts known by me or props. known by me to be probable.

The simple objection to all these forms is that if "true" meant this, no belief *could* be true unless there were a considerable number of other facts & believed props. with wh. it was coherent; whereas quite plainly it *could* be. A belief might & would be true, provided p, even if the person in question had no other belief & knew no facts. I daresay it may be true that every actual truth always *is* coherent with many others; but it's quite clear it *could* be without.

As for pragmatist theories of truth, it's again extremely difficult to define any precisely, & they usually are mixed up with theories of the test of truth. The formula is that "true" = "works", wh. may mean ever so many different things.

Yet *all* forms of it can be simply refuted as inconsistent with our 3 props.; bec. "what *works*" includes "has *some* relation to some subsequent events". It would then be *impossible*, if truth means this, that anything should be true, if there were *no* subsequent events; but it's clearly *not* impossible.

The next Epistemological question I want to touch on is one wh. you may think at first sight has nothing to do with *knowledge*, in our sense, but in fact has.

It is the question usually put in the form: Is there a test or criterion of truth? & if so, what is it? Or often: What is the test of truth? assuming that there is one.

I think people often take this to be a question *not* concerned with knowledge, because they adopt the false view that to say

ϕ is a *positive* criterion of truth is merely to say

ϕ is a property other than truth itself

& either (1) every prop. (or judgment) wh. has ϕ is true

or (2) every prop. wh. has ϕ is true, & also every true prop. has ϕ.

If this were so, then a property wh. satisfied (1) would be a test of *some* truth, & one wh. satisfied (2) would be a universal criterion of truth.

And ϕ is a *negative* criterion of truth

ϕ is a property other than falsehood

& either (1) everything wh. has ϕ is false

or (2) everything wh. has ϕ is false, & everything wh. is false has ϕ.

Being self-contradictory satisfies (1).

But in fact "criterion" never means merely this.

In order that ϕ may be a positive criterion of truth, it's necessary that it should not only be a property such that every prop. wh. possesses it is true, but a property such that by finding that a prop. possesses it we are able to find out that it is true. I.e. we must be able to know that a prop. possesses it *before* we know that it is true; & hence to infer that it is true.

Now that there are properties belonging *only* to true props., such that we can do this, is certain: e.g. that of following from a true prop.

But when people talk of a ⟨the⟩ *universal* test of truth, they mean: A property (other than truth) such that *both* when we first know it to belong to a prop., we know that prop. to be true; & also *only* when . . . .

And it's *impossible* that there should be a universal criterion of truth: since whatever ϕ may be, we shall have to *know* that it's true our prop. has ϕ, before we can use it. It can't be the case that in the case of *every* prop. we know to be true we can know it to be so, *only* if we first know some other prop. to be true.

In other words the prop. that there is a universal test of truth is really identical with the false prop. that *all* knowledge is derivative. It's perfectly certain that there are some things we know *immediately*, i.e. *not* bec. of our knowing something else, wh. is our evidence for them.

Hence neither coherence nor working *can* be universal test of truth.

PART III

SELECTIONS FROM A COURSE OF LECTURES GIVEN IN 1933–34

L

I

WHAT IS ANALYSIS?

You no doubt have some conception of what philos. is—otherwise you wouldn't be here—but it's quite a different thing saying what you mean by doing philos. And it is a matter of some importance to try to get clear as to what one is trying to do if one tries to do philos. And it's a matter of extreme difficulty to give a precise def. of philos.: I have to confess I'm very vague; but I will try to be as definite as I can. It's very hard, & I shall very likely be wrong. But I think there are some things worth saying.

You see the general question we've got to try to answer is one which it's most natural to put in the form: What *is* Philosophy? But this means the same as: How is the word philosophy in one of its senses used *now*? What is the modern English usage?

And I think it's important to insist that what we want to discuss is how it's used *now*. And it doesn't mean now "the love of wisdom" even if it once did. Bec. there is I think no doubt that at one time it was used differently. Newton's *Principia* was called a work on Natural Philosophy: but nobody would think of saying now that in stating the Law of Gravitation Newton was making a philosophical prop., though they would say that in that book he does mix up philosophical props. with scientific, e.g. in what he says about Absolute Space & Absolute Time. In the 17th & 18th century "philosophy" was used in such a sense that it included what we now call Natural Science.

Now it's *not* the case merely that people used "philosophy" in the same sense as we do now, but took a different view as to what questions were philosophical. People often use language which seems to imply this. Thus it is held that when Physics became thoroughly established, it ceased to be regarded as philosophy; & that later the same happened or is happening to Psychology. And it is sometimes suggested that "philosophy" means only the unscientific treatment of any subject whatever; & that when scientific methods of treating all subjects are discovered, people will have discovered that *no* questions are philos. questions.

What really happens is that the name "philosophy" has changed

153

its meaning: & probably that will still go on happening to some extent.

We mustn't assume then that it meant the same as it does now; & what we want to know is what it means *now*.

And to this the first answer is that it's still used in several different senses: you all know the sense in wh. it is used when it is said that a person bears misfortune with philosophy or that he's of a philosophical temperament. It means roughly that he's not unduly disturbed. Of course, that's not the sense we're concerned with.

The sense we are concerned with is the sense in which it's used when we talk about books on philosophy: the sense in which it's used when in a bookseller's catalogue books are classified as books on philosophy. There is a *pretty clear* distinction here: there are a good many books with regard to wh. there might be a doubt whether they are on philosophy; but there are lots about wh. there's no doubt at all that they are, & lots where there's no doubt at all that they aren't.

On what does it depend whether a book is a book on philosophy or not?

There are questions or problems of a certain kind, such that a book which tries to give the answer to questions of that kind will be on philosophy, & a book which doesn't won't be.

I'm not sure that this is quite satisfactory. I think it may be that there are some questions such that a book which tries to answer them by one kind of method will be philos., & a book wh. tries to answer them by another won't be: & perhaps there are *none* such that a book will be philosophy if it tries to answer them *whatever* method it uses.

But there are sorts of questions, such that a book *won't* be philosophy, unless it's about questions of that sort: although perh. to be about them isn't sufficient to make it philos.

I'm going to begin by trying to say: What sort of questions are such that a book which tries to answer them *may* be philosophical?

The difficulty of answering the question what philos. is, largely consists in the fact that there are so many different kinds of questions of all of which we can say that a book which is about them, provided it discusses them in an appropriate way, is about philos. How can we get a general description which applies to all of them, & applies to no questions which aren't philosophical questions?

In order to get at some idea what sort of questions do satisfy this description, I'm going to take a classification of Prof. Broad's (Contemp. Phil. I, p. 82)[1] which attempts to make a distinction wh. is, I think, in its broad outlines central.

Broad begins by saying that under the name "Phil." there seem to him to be included 2 very different subjects, which are pursued by different methods & can expect to reach quite different degrees of certainty, & which he is in the habit of calling "Critical" & "Speculative Phil.". He implies that if you are doing philos. at all, you must be doing one or the other or both: so that, if he's right, then if we've got a complete account of the sort of questions dealt with by each, we shall have a complete account of the sort of questions wh. are philos. questions.

I said there are certain sorts of questions, such that you *won't* be doing philosophy, unless you are trying to discover the right answer to one of them; though, perhaps, even if you are trying to find the right answer to one of them, it won't follow that you are doing phil., unless you are trying to find it in certain ways.

And in order to answer the question: What is philosophy? part of what you've got to do is try to give a general description of *all* the sorts of questions such that you won't be doing philos. unless you are trying to answer a question of that sort.

I said this is very difficult bec. there seem to be such an immense number of different sorts of questions, such that, provided you are using an appropriate method, you will be doing philos. if you are trying to find the right answer to one of them.

But I said Broad has tried to give a classification of them—or of some of the chief—in dividing philosophy into Critical & Speculative, & then trying to describe 2 sorts of questions which belong to Critical, & what sort belong to Speculative.

And we saw that first sort he says belongs to Critical is the *analysis* of certain sorts of *concepts*. He only describes *what* sorts, by saying they must be very *general* concepts which are constantly used both in ordinary life & in the special sciences, & giving as examples number, thing, quality, change, cause. He

---

[1] [C. D. Broad, "Critical and Speculative Philosophy" in J. H. Muirhead (ed.), *Contemporary British Philosophy. First Series* (London, 1924).]

implies that if, by appropriate methods, you are trying to find the right answer to the question: Is so-&-so a right analysis of the concept "cause"? you will be doing philosophy. And implies, as I think quite rightly, that a great part of what philosophers have actually done, when everybody would say they were doing philos., has consisted in trying to find the answer to questions of this sort.

Now I gave a simple example to shew one sort of thing which I thought he meant by "giving an analysis of a concept".

I said if you say or write up

x is brother of y *means* x is male & x & y had a common parent

you are giving an analysis of a concept—though, in this case, not of the sort of concept which it is the business of philosophy to analyse, perhaps because the concept in question is not so general as to be constantly used not only in ordinary life but in *all* the special sciences: it isn't, for instance, used at all in physics & chemistry.

But I think Broad would say that if you made a statement about the word "cause", just of this kind, you would be giving an analysis of the concept of "cause".

E.g. x caused y means x preceded y & whenever an event like x has been observed it has also been observed that an event like y followed the event in question.

I'm quite sure this is *not* what x caused y means, but this *would* be an analysis though not a correct one.

I want to say a little more about this sort of analysis, because I want to point out certain things about it, & in particular to distinguish it from some other sorts which I think are equally, if not more important, in philos.

Now such statements are statements to the effect that a certain word or phrase has a certain meaning; but they differ from some statements to this effect in a respect which I want to state as carefully as possible, namely this:

They are statements with regard to a word or expression, W, such that in making the statement you *use* another verbal expression, with regard to which, in making the statement, you *either say* or *imply* that it has the same meaning as W.

E.g. if you say

x is brother of y means x is male & has a common parent with y you are using the [latter] expression & are certainly implying, if you are not saying, that this has the same meaning as "is brother of";

e.g. that the Duke of Connaught was a brother of King Edward means the same as

the Duke of Connaught was male & had a common parent with [King Edward].

Everybody would so understand your statement. But now I have said, *either* say or imply. Which is it?

There are people, e.g. Johnson, p. 90[1], who say that

all you are saying is that "is brother of" means the same as "is male & has a common parent with".

I think this is certainly *not* all you are saying: if it were all, you would not be telling anyone *what* the meaning of "brother" is, but merely saying either (1) that it had *some* meaning wh. the other expression also had or (2) that the latter had only one meaning, & that brother had the meaning which this had. If this were all, it is an assertion you might make, even if you hadn't the least idea what the latter meant, & were not attaching any meaning to it, & were not therefore mentioning any meaning it had, & saying the first had that. But this is certainly not what you are doing: you are making an assertion which you could not be making unless you were attaching some meaning to "male" & to "has a common parent with" & to the form of combination.

That this is so, I think is also proved by the fact that you would be saying exactly the same thing, if you said

x is brother of y means x est mâle et . . .

You would be saying the *same* thing, though you used different words to express it; & so you would if you said: x & y had either the same mother or the same father as y or both, or said this in French.

And this, I think, shews also that it is no *part* of what you are saying, since you would *not* be asserting the same thing in the 2 cases if you were talking about the right-hand expression.

Look here

(1) "is brother of" means the same as "is male & had a common parent with"

is *not* the same prop. as

[1] [W. E. Johnson, *Logic*, Part I (Cambridge, 1921).]

(2) "is brother of" means the same as "is male & either had the same mother or the same father or both".

But the 2 expressions (a) "is brother of" means is male & had a common parent with

& (b) "is brother of" means is male & either had same mother or same father as or both

do express the same prop. (the one prop. is the same as the other) & hence it can't be the case that (1) is a part of what's asserted by (a) & (2) of what's asserted by (b).

Moreover (1) doesn't follow from (a) nor (2) from (b).

⟨Although (a) implies (1)—from the supposition that you've expressed *yourself correctly* & that what you say is true, it will follow.⟩

This means that almost everything Johnson says about def. is wrong, & the same applies to a good many other people.

Now you *can* make statements to the effect that a certain word or expression has a certain meaning, without using another *verbal* expression with regard to which you are implying that it has the same meaning.

Suppose a schoolboy asks you: What colour does "rouge" mean? You could answer simply by pointing, & saying: "That's the colour it means"; or "That colour".

Johnson uses the phrase "ostensive def." for the kind of thing you are doing when you explain the meaning of a word by making a statement of this sort; & you *can* do it without making a state-ment at all—by simply pointing. (You are here asserting some-thing, therefore perhaps making a prop., but you can hardly be said to be *making a statement*.)

Our def. of "brother" is not therefore merely a statement to the effect that "brother" has a certain meaning: it is a statement of this sort, which is not of the sort which Johnson calls an *ostensive def.*

It is of the sort which J. calls a "bi-verbal def." & I believe that what I have given is an exact def. of what J. means by this phrase (not what he thinks he means).

But now our statement differs in an important way from some "bi-verbal defs."—with this meaning.

J. gives as an instance "valour means courage": he might have given "rouge means red": these are bi-verbal defs. in the sense defined, though I think it's a mistake to call them defs.

How does ours differ from these?

In the fact that the phrase used on the right-hand side, which is the one with regard to which it is implied that it means the same as the one on the left, is a more complex phrase than the one on the left, in the sense that there occur in it a greater number of symbols to each of which a separate meaning is attached. "Brother" is a *simple* symbol in the sense defined by Russell in *Introd.*[1], p. 173: it has parts, but no parts wh. are themselves on this occasion used as symbols. In our def. the right-hand has more parts which are themselves symbols in that usage.

When we give a def. of this kind, I say we are giving an *analytic def.*

You can I think be said to give a def., without giving an analytic one.

Johnson, p. 108, contends that this is so; & *one* of his examples seems to me really to be a definition & *not* an analytic one.

"*l* is the *logarithm* of p to the *base* b" means $b^l = p$.

So far as I can see this is exactly like defining

x is a grandparent of y means y is a grandchild of x

which isn't analytic: is it a def.?

x is grandparent of y means There's somebody of whom x is parent, & y is child, is analytic.

A statement that a certain word or phrase W has a certain meaning, when the statement is such that, in making it, you're giving an analytic def. of W, is an analysis of a concept, *provided* W *does stand for a concept.*

But now when we say "brother" means . . ., by "means" we may mean "always means" or "sometimes means" or "most commonly means".

You *can* say each of these things, & whichever you are doing you'll be defining a word & analysing a concept.

But you'll all of you see that, if you *do* say the first, you're almost certain to be wrong, since there are hardly any words which are used in one sense only.

"Brother" isn't, "number" isn't, "thing" isn't, "quality" isn't, & though I can't say for certain "cause" isn't, I think it's extremely unlikely.

Consequently if you want to give a *true* analytic def. of "number", you'll have to say merely "number" sometimes means

[1] [B. Russell, *Introduction to Mathematical Philosophy* (London, 1919).]

so-&-so, e.g. cardinal number, ordinal number, or most often means so-&-so. Or you can say: In this usage.

And if this is all you say, what concept are you analysing?

Not the concept "number", but *one* of the concepts for which "number" stands.

I've said this bec. I don't want you to be misled by people's talking of analysing *the* concept "number" etc., into thinking you ever will be doing this. You'll only be analysing *one* of a number of concepts; or of course you may try to analyse several.

For this reason I don't like this way of talking of analysing *the* concept, as if each word always stood for the same concept. Of course, there's no harm in it, if it's understood that all that is meant is analysing *one* of the concepts for wh. "number" stands.

Broad I think talks, here, only of analysis of *concepts*; but I think, before we leave this section of Critical Phil., it should be mentioned that there's another thing some philosophers do, which is called analysis & is very similar to what we've been considering, but which is not analysis of a *concept* at all.

Take Russell's *Theory of Definite Descriptions*: this consists in giving an analysis, & an analysis in a very similar sense to what we've been considering: it is considered by many to be important: nobody doubts that it's philosophy, though some, e.g. Mr Joseph, apparently think it's bad philosophy, & is untrue: but that may be bec. they haven't understood what R. is saying: & yet so far as I can see it's *not* analysis of a concept at all. Ramsey calls it a paradigm of phil.

Let's see how it differs from, & resembles, the kind of analysis we've been considering. (I may possibly *not* give the essence of it.)

R. tells us one thing (I'm not going to use his exact words, because I don't want to be bothered by irrelevant considerations)—

he tells us that the *words* "The present King of England is more than 60 years old" if used in the ordinary way

mean

"There's at least one person of whom the following 3 things are all true viz. (1) that the person in question is at present a King of England (2) that nobody except the person in question is at present a King of England & (3) that the person in question is more than 60 years old."

He expresses this more neatly by saying

There is an x such that (1) x is at present a King of England,

(2) nobody but x is at present a King of England & (3) x is more than 60 years old.

And he explains further that this is equivalent to saying:

At least one person could be found, pointing at whom you could say truly: This person is at present King of England; Nobody but this person is . . .; & This person is more than 60 years old.

Or finally

that at least one conjunctive prop. of the form

(1) x is at present King of E., (2) nobody but x is & (3) x is more than 60 years old, is true.

Now all this seems to me obviously true.

Has R. been analysing any *concept*?

He has, & he says so, been analysing a *prop.*, bec. he has been saying that words wh. *express* a prop., mean so-&-so.

What concept has he been analysing? If any "The present King of England"? But is that a concept? I doubt if anyone would say so.

But moreover the analysis of *this* prop. doesn't constitute the theory of definite descriptions: this is only an *example*.

What the theory of descriptions says is

Expressions *of the form*

"The thing which is ϕ, is F"

mean

There is at least one x, such that (1) x is ϕ, (2) nothing but x is ϕ & (3) x is F.

What *concept* is being analysed here? No concept: you're merely giving one meaning of a *form of expression*, not of a word which means a concept.

You might say, & R. does sometimes talk as if this were so, that you're saying what the meaning of the word "the" is: & perhaps this is true; but nobody would say "the" stands for a concept.

Now this is obviously very similar to the sort of thing we did in the case of brother, & yet it's *not* an analysis of a concept. It is def. & it is analytic def.; but there's no one word such that it was a phrase on the *right*-hand that you imply has the same meaning as that word.

How does it differ?

(1) It doesn't use in the case of any one word or phrase, which

occurs in ever so many different props., another phrase which could be substituted for that one: it only tells you how "the author of Wav.", "the present King of England" can be translated.

(2) R. apparently holds that even when you are considering a single prop. like the King of England [etc.], you use no phrase in the right-hand expression which *means* the same as the one on the left.

You're not using an expression, with regard to which you imply that it has the same meaning.

This is why he calls "the present King of England" an incomplete symbol.

Finally, I think, it's worth noticing that this resembles the last in that, if you say

Expressions of the form

"The thing which is ϕ, is F"

mean

There is at least one x such that . . .

you will only be saying something true, if you say *sometimes* mean, or *generally* mean, not *always* mean.

That is you're only giving one *meaning* of the form of expression, not *the* meaning; just as in the case of "brother" you're only analysing *one* of the concepts meant, not *the* concept.

R. often speaks as if he were giving *the* meaning of the form of expression

"The thing which is ϕ, is F":

but he isn't.

"The right arm is often slightly longer than the left" if you analysed this in that way you'd find you were asserting that there's only one right arm in the world.

Now I've mentioned 2 sorts of analysis, both of which consist in giving one of the meanings of a word or phrase, *or* a form of expression, & giving it in one particular way.

But I don't think I ought to leave the subject without mentioning one other kind of analysis, wh. doesn't seem to me quite the same as either of these; which resembles (2) more than (1)[1]; but which may perhaps be said to give an analysis of a concept.

The 2 problems of philos. which I think interest me most, & also puzzle me most, are instances of this 3rd kind.

[1] [I.e. the kind of analysis exemplified by Russell's Theory of Descriptions rather than that exemplified by the case of "brother".]

One is this:

Consider the prop.

"I am nearer to this blackboard than any of you are".

This is a prop. which we all understand perfectly well & you can all see that it's true, & yet it seems to me fearfully puzzling to see *what its analysis is* in a certain respect.

The point of difficulty is this. It seems to me perfectly clear that when I say this I'm saying something about a percept or sensation or sense-datum or sensum which I have at the moment. But there's every reason to think that this isn't identical even with the surface of the blackboard, far less with the blackboard: that I'm not saying of it that I'm nearer to it than you are. Yet somehow the statement about the blackboard which I make is identical with a statement about it. What sort of statement about it is it identical with?

This is similar to (2) in respect that, of course, it's not the analysis of *this* particular prop. we want to know; it's only used as an example of millions of others; & it differs from (2) in that it's much more difficult to say *what* others—of what form. You can only say: All expressions in which you use "this" or "that" to refer to a physical thing or material thing which you are at the moment perceiving. The question is as to how "this" is used in such cases.

And I think this *may* be the way of giving an analysis of the concept "material thing".

Another problem of the same sort is how I use "I" in this prop. This is a problem to wh. James was giving an answer when he said "The present thought is the only thinker". This doesn't *sound* like an analysis: but I think if you try to see what it means, it is doing nothing except to say something about one way in which the word "I" is used. What it seems to say is this: that when I say "I am thinking of James' doctrine that the present thought is the only thinker", I could substitute for "I", "the present thought". If this were exactly what it meant, I think it would certainly be wrong. I think it is saying that we could substitute for "I am thinking about" a phrase about the present thought, not that it *thinks*, but such that "the present thought is engaged *about*" means the same as "I am thinking about", although neither does "the present thought" = "I" nor "is engaged about" = "is thinking about". Of course this wouldn't

be supposed to give the meaning of "I am nearer this blackboard":
that would mean "The body which *belongs* to this present thought"
& we should have to try to get clear as to what "belongs to" here
means. The concept of the "subject" or (a barbarism) the Self.
I am a Self = when I use the word "I" it has this kind of meaning.

II

THE JUSTIFICATION OF ANALYSIS

So far I've been saying that so far as the business of philos. consists in Analysis, it seems to consist in trying to find, with regard to certain kinds of words or phrases, & certain *forms of expression*, true statements of the form "the phrase, W, or the form of expression, Z, *sometimes* means so-&-so", where the part of the statement which follows "means" *uses another* phrase or expression, which is more *complex* than the one of which you are stating that it means so-&-so. I emphasized that where what it tries to give the meaning of is not a word or phrase, but a form of expression, it can't in general be said to be giving an analysis of a *concept*; & that therefore B. doesn't seem to me to give a complete account in suggesting that the part of Critical Phil. which consists in *analysis* is only analysis of concepts. And I'm not at all sure that it isn't part of the business of this part of philosophy to give explanations about the meaning of words wh. are not analyses, e.g. to say that they're indefinable, & *then* say more about them.

It seems therefore that part of the object of philosophy is merely to make props. about the meaning of words & phrases & forms of expression (only of course certain *kinds* of props. about their meaning, & certain *kinds* of words, phrases & forms of expression); and it may seem that this is a very humble thing to aim at, & a very uninteresting thing: that an answer to the question what a word means, can't be nearly so interesting as answers to questions which are *not* about the meaning of words: that so far as this goes philosophy compares very unfavourably with other studies which try to find & succeed in finding correct answers to questions wh. are *not* merely about the meaning of words or forms of expression.

So I want to say something about what is the *use* of trying to find answers to this sort of question especially as I think that the most important part of philos. is of this kind.

And first of all, it's well to emphasize that it certainly hasn't got the use which finding out the meaning of a word has, when for instance you are learning a foreign language. To find out the meaning of a word, of which you don't already know the meaning,

can, of course, be of use in helping you to understand sentences
in which that word occurs: it may help you to read a foreign book,
or to understand a foreigner when he speaks to you, & also to
make yourself understood by him. But this is not the use of
philosophic definition; *because* they're all of them definitions of
words or forms of expression *you already understand*—you
already *know* their meaning, in the sense that you *attach the
common meanings* to them when you use them or hear or read them,
though you mayn't *know their meanings* in the sense of being able
to make true props. of the form "this *means* so-&-so". Of course,
in philosophy there do occur defs. of technical terms, or technical
usages of old terms, which do serve the purpose of helping you to
understand sentences in wh. those words are used. But these
defs. of new terms, or new usages, are *not* part of what is meant
by analysis in phil. nor is it any part of the ultimate object of
philos. to give them. That is exclusively concerned with giving
defs. of words & forms of expression which you already understand: this is said, when Broad says that what philos. tries to
analyse is concepts which you *use* in ordinary life.

⟨To use a concept for wh. a word stands = to use the word,
& attach a certain meaning to the word.⟩

What can be the use of finding out or trying to find out that a
word, which you already understand, means so-&-so?

Now 2 things are said about the use of this, which don't come
to exactly the same thing.

(1) It is said that it helps to make your thoughts *clearer*—that
it helps you to think clearly.

(2) It is said that you are liable to be puzzled by certain sentences
in which you find these words used, & that philosophic analysis
will prevent you from being puzzled in these cases, or at least
will make you less puzzled.

Thus B. says: There is need for C.P. because those concepts
wh. it tries to analyse really are "obscure", & because their
obscurity really does lead to difficulties—the kind of difficulty he
has in mind being that we are puzzled by certain questions or
statements in wh. the words are used; a puzzlement which he
says is certainly due in part to the fact that we're not *clear as to
what we mean by certain words*.

He seems then to distinguish 2 objects of Crit. Phil.: (1) the
getting clearer, (2) the being freed from puzzles. One object of

the getting clearer is to get rid of the puzzles, but only one. And of course it might be that it's worth while to get clear, quite apart from being freed from the puzzles.

(1) As to clearness I don't doubt that phil. analys. *can* help to make *some* of your thoughts clearer in some sense: and that this is *part* of its object.

But I think it's worth asking the question: On what occasions does it make them clearer?

I want to distinguish 4 different kinds of occasions on wh. it might be supposed it does.

(a) It must be remembered that the words & forms of expression, of wh. this part of phil. tells us that they sometimes have certain meanings, are words which we *use* in ordinary life & which those who pursue the special sciences use in them.

So it might be asked: Does phil. anal. have the result that, *whenever* you *use* the word or form of expression defined. in ordinary life or in the special sciences, the thought you express by the sentence in which you use it is a clearer one? Has philosophy *this* bearing on life & the sciences?

I think some philosophers have suggested that it does have, & ought to have this effect, & that the main or sole object of phil. is to have it. But, so far as I can see, it doesn't in fact make any difference at all to the clearness of your thoughts on most occasions when you use the word. E.g. I have been familiar for many years with R.'s Theory of Descrs., but I don't believe that on most occasions when I use & read & hear expressions of the form "The so-&-so", my thoughts are any clearer than they were before, or than are those of people who have never heard of the theory of Descrs. I understand such expressions in general in exactly the same way, & with exactly the same degree of clearness, as I did before. And similarly even if I could get a satisfactory answer to my question as to the use of "this blackboard" or of "I", I don't believe it would make any difference to the way I used such expressions in ordinary life. I should still go on using such expressions as "I'm nearer the blackboard than you are" in exactly the same way I do now & as I should have before I began phil.; & with the same degree of clearness. My thought in a way is *now* very clear; & it wouldn't in general be a bit the clearer for my having found the answer to the 2 philos. problems. And I believe the same is true of such terms in the special sciences.

M

I don't therefore think that one of the uses of philos. is to have this sort of far-reaching effect on your use of the words defined in ordinary life or in the special sciences.

(b) On some occasions when you use these words in ordinary life, you use them in a process of reasoning or in an argument, & it may be said that on this sort of occasion, the philosophical analysis will prevent your adopting false conclusions through confusion. And I think something wh. prob. B. had in mind in talking of analysis may possibly have some little effect on these occasions in *preventing confusion*. Only here I think it is not strictly the def., as we have defined it, which has the effect, but the having discovered with regard to a given word that it *sometimes* means this, *sometimes* that. Confused argument & reasoning in ordinary life or the sciences generally results, I think, from failing to distinguish *different* senses in which a word or expression is used: & merely to know it's *sometimes* used in this sense won't help you, unless you know it's *also* sometimes used in others. *Distinguishing* of different senses, wh. philosophers do do, is not to be confused with the *analysis* of some one sense. And it's the former wh. is most likely to be useful. And, of course, you *can* distinguish without giving an analysis: you can say: In *this* sense part of what you are saying is so-&-so, in this other case not.

On the whole I think what philos. analysis can do in this way is very little; & this is certainly not the main justification of philos. —that it makes arguments & reasoning in ordinary life or the sciences less confused.

The same, I think, is true of the special sciences.

(c) If I'm right, the chief use of analysis in the way of clearness, is only clearness which it produces when *you're doing philos. itself*.

And here I think we've got to distinguish 2 things

(α) The sort of clearness you have in understanding the def. itself

(β) The sort of clearness which understanding a given def. may give you in understanding other *philos. props.*—either another def., or a philos. prop. of the kind we're going to consider which is *not* a def.

I think it has both these kinds of effects, & that this is its main object.

To say that (α) is our main object, is, I think, to say that it's worth while finding out these defs. for its own sake. This is what I do really think. I think it's a mistake to think even of this part of philos. as mainly useful for the sake of *something else*. Many people certainly are interested in these problems of def. for their own sake: and I should be inclined to say it's not much use your doing philos. unless you *are*. And I think not only *are* people interested in these for their own sake; but they are right to be: the sort of clearness you enjoy when you arrive at a good def. of this sort of word or form of expression is, it seems to me, something worth having for its own sake.

(β) No doubt it's worth having for the sake of the clearness it may bring on *other* philos. props.: but if *other* defs., only if that's worth having for its own sake. No doubt it *does* help with props. that aren't defs.—in the solution of puzzles, wh. aren't merely puzzles as to what a word means: & some people no doubt are chiefly interested in these others. People say you must have a clear notion what a question means before you can answer it. But *philos.* clearness is not necess. to answer such a question as: Am I nearer the blackboard than you are? And does it really help to answer *philos.* props.? I doubt if it helps you at all to say whether they are true; but only to see more clearly what the question means.

I want now to say something about what sort of difficulties, in the form of *puzzles*, it helps to remove.

Here too I think it's only *philosophical* puzzles that it helps to remove, & here again chiefly I think by *distinguishing* senses of words or forms of expression rather than strictly by analysis. And it's no use at all, in this way, unless it's worth while *for its own sake* to be free from these puzzles.

Broad gives 2 illustrations of puzzles, which he thinks philos. analysis will help to remove; & I think it's worth while considering them, in order to see what sort of thing it really can do, or can be thought to do. (And to bring out the point that it's only *philos.* puzzles that it helps us to solve.)

His first example is: Suppose we are asked: "In what place is the mirror image of a pin? And is it in this place in the same sense in which the pin itself is in *its* place?"

He says we find ourselves puzzled by such questions; & suggests our puzzlement will certainly partly be removed, if Critical Philosophy gives us an analysis of what's meant by "being in a place". And he seems to assume that it's certainly worth while to have this puzzlement removed.

Let's consider this example in a little detail to see what sort of use he is claiming that Crit. Phil. is, & *how* it effects this useful result.

In the first place: *Are* you puzzled? I think I must admit I am in a way, in spite of all the Critical Phil. I've done. But I'm not sure my puzzlement is all of the sort B. means: it seems such a queer question to ask: why should you ask it?

But supposing you are puzzled, is it at all worth while to get rid of that particular kind of puzzle?

And in favour of the view that it isn't, it might be urged that you hardly ever are asked questions of that sort; nobody but a philosopher would think of asking them; & why shouldn't you be content just to be puzzled, on the rare occasions when you are asked them? Is it at all desirable that you should be saved by Crit. Phil. from an experience which so rarely occurs?

In order to carry the matter a little further, I'll give the sort of answer wh. I think a correct Critical Phil. would give to this question.

In *what* place.

It isn't in *any* place at all, in the sense in which the pin itself is in a place: bec. when you say the pin is in a place, you mean that it's in a place in *physical* space, e.g. lying on your toilet-table, & in a place near the middle of it. The image simply isn't in physical space at all: it's not at any distance in any direction from the toilet-table. So that if by "In what place" you mean: In what place in physical space? The answer is in *none*. And this is what we often do mean: e.g. Where is Broad now? (If Russell's Critical Phil. in *Analysis of Matter* were right this answer would be wrong, since he says that the answer is "It's in your head". By this he should mean in your head in the same sense in which your brain is in your head & in which the blackboard is in this room: and if he does he's certainly wrong. Of course he may be able to define a sense in wh. it may be said to be in your head, but it won't be the same sense in wh. one physical thing can be said to be *in* another. The sort of thing Critical Phil. really can do is to explain why R. is wrong when he says this: & if you don't find that question interesting, I think you'd better not do Crit. Phil. It is simply nonsense to say it's in your head in that sense.)

But now in saying it's not in *any* place in *physical* space, one's implying that there's perhaps another space, in which it is in a place. And there certainly is in a philosophic sense of space & place, namely your visual field at the moment—visual space or your visual space. It certainly will be at *a* place in this space, though you may not be able to answer at *what* place: if you could say the middle point of the line is in the *exact* centre of my visual field, that would answer in what place: & so would the middle point is exactly equidistant from sense-data of 2 sides of mirror, & of top & bottom.

The place in your visual field at which it is, is not identical with any place in physical space.

Now this shews that there's an *ambiguity* in "in a place"— 2 different senses (but not in its ordinary sense); so that it's not really *one concept* you're analysing, but 2 different concepts: & of course, what philosophers often are doing is pointing out 2 different senses in wh. words are used, which are liable to be confused.

And the problem of *analysing* one of these, when you've got it clear, is rather a different problem. That the image isn't *anywhere*, in the ordinary sense, is a quite clear prop.: just as it's a clear prop. that there aren't any unicorns *anywhere*.

I say this bec. B. suggests that it's only where we're *not* clear about the meaning of a word, that it's worth the while of Crit. Phil. to analyse. But in fact some of its chief problems are in analysing [statements] which are quite clear. "There's a storey in this building above us", "This isn't the top storey" are perfectly clear; yet one of the main problems of Critical Phil. is to give an analysis of this kind of statement.

About the 2nd part of Broad's question: this is not a question of analysis of an ordinary meaning of "is a place"; but of explaining a philosophic meaning.

We've said it's in a *place* in a different *space*. But is a *place* in one space, a place in the *same sense* as a place in the other? And further, whether it is or not, is what's meant by being *in* that place the same in the 2 cases?

I *think* that the answer is that it's 2 different senses of "place", & that therefore "in" means something different too. If, as many philosophers think, the meaning of place were the same, so would be the meaning of "in".

III

QUESTIONS OF SPECULATIVE PHILOSOPHY

What other kinds of questions than questions about the meanings of words does philos. try to answer?

Broad distinguishes 2 kinds, one of wh. he assigns to Critical, the other to Speculative: but I said it wasn't clear to me why some of those he assigns to Critical shouldn't be assigned to Spec. And I'm not going to follow him in detail or try to find out exactly what he means; but merely to try to give some sort of classification of questions *other* than Analysis, wh. it seems to me philosophers do try to answer.

(1) "Discuss questions about the nature of Reality as a whole."

This is obviously very vague; but some philosophers certainly have discussed questions which come under this head: & I want to try to give some idea what kind of questions coming under this head phils. try to answer.

⟨You might think it must mean discussing props. of the form "Nothing is real but so-&-so".

And some philos. have actually put forward props. of this form, or been supposed to do so.

E.g. some have been supposed to say: (1) Nothing is real but matter (Materialism), although I think nobody has ever really held this in its natural meaning, i.e. there's no such thing as Mind: for it turns out that they've not been denying Mind, but merely suggesting a particular *analysis* of props. like "I see . . .", "I think . . ." (e.g. Behaviourism). So that part at least of what appeared at first sight to be a prop. *not* about the meaning of words, is in fact *merely* about the meaning of words.

(2) Nothing is real but a single experience (Bradley). I think this has some meaning, & is *not* merely a question of analysis.

(3) Nothing is real but my own experience; or even my own present experience (Solipsism).

Has anybody ever really held this? People confuse it with: Nothing is *known* to be real, which has really been held.

The other thing has I think only been held where it is really a question of *analysis*. They don't *deny* that other people have had *experiences*, but only say that to say that they had is to say something about my own experience.

So of the present moment: not deny that I had past, but that it is saying something of a particular sort about my present.⟩

(2) The second thing I want to take from Broad is his saying that one question which it is the business of phil. to discuss is the question whether "Every change has a cause". But this he puts not under Speculative but under the second part of Critical Philos.

Now isn't the prop. that "Every change has a cause" a prop. about the (nature of) Reality as a whole?

I should have thought it was; & I should have thought people generally would have said so. At all events I'm going to use "about the nature of Reality as a whole" in a vague sense wh. includes this.

It looks, therefore, as if Broad really wished to divide questions about reality as a whole into 2 groups (1) those which he says belong to Speculative Phil., (2) others, like "Every change has a cause", which *don't*.

What is the difference between these 2 groups?

Now a distinction, which does seem to me of very great importance, is suggested by one thing that B. says about "Every change has a cause".

He says, & that is apparently part of his reason for including it under Critical not under Speculative, that "*we always* assume it". He gives it as an instance of a class of very *fundamental* props. which are *uncritically* assumed both in science & daily life: we might take "uncritically" in the case of the sciences, & perhaps "assumed" too, to mean that they are not among the props. which the sciences try to *prove*. Just as his first part of Crit. Phil. consisted in the analysis of concepts, which we constantly use both in the sciences & ordinary life but wh. are not defined in the sciences; so this second part consists in the criticism of fundamental props. which are always assumed in both, but which the sciences don't attempt to prove. How B. describes the kind of criticism which philos. has to apply to these is that "it has to expose them to every objection we can think of ourselves or find in the writings of others".

I.e. we've got to try to discover whether there's any reason at all to believe them, & if so how much. And there's no doubt that this describes something wh. philos. have tried to do.

Now I'm not at all sure that we do always assume both in ordinary life & in the sciences this particular fundamental prop. that every change has a cause. Perhaps there is some sense of "assume" in which we always do: I don't know.

But I think B. is right that there are a number of very fundamental props., which may be said to [be] props. about Reality as a whole, which philosophers have criticised & which it is considered the proper business of philos. to criticize, of which it is true that they are in a certain sense, which I will try to define (though perh. it's not what B. meant by assumed) constantly *assumed* by all of us both in ordinary life & in the sciences.

We may, therefore, I think, make a fundamental distinction, which I think is very important & is also very striking if you look at the actual works of philosophers, between 2 kinds of questions, about reality as a whole, which philosophers have discussed.

(1) Questions about reality as a whole, to which one particular answer is "assumed" or "presupposed" (in a sense I have yet to define) by *us all* both in ordinary life & in the special sciences.

(2) Questions about reality as a whole, to which *no* answer is assumed or presupposed by us all either in ordinary life or in the special sciences. I think perhaps it was the discussion of this kind of question wh. B. was mainly thinking of as constituting Speculative Phil. So far as philosophers give answers to this sort of question, they would be saying something which was neither presupposed by Common knowledge nor by the sciences, nor in *conflict* with it. And I think a good many philosophers have aimed at answering questions of this sort. Props. of this sort are, I think, "That God exists" (this I think would always be taken to be a prop. about reality as a whole); or Spinoza's that there are an infinite number of other *attributes beside extension & thought*; or Leibniz's "that this is the best of all possible worlds". So far as this is the kind of question he is thinking of, you can see, I think, why he holds that the degree of certainty attainable, at all events at present, is not very high.

I said that, if we consider what sorts of philosophical questions there are which are *not* merely questions about the meanings of words & *are* questions about the nature of Reality as a whole, I thought we could divide questions of this sort into 2 great divisions, which I distinguished as (1) questions to which one

particular answer is "assumed" both by us all in ordinary life &
by scientists in pursuing their special sciences—the same answer
both by us in ordinary life & by the scientists, & (2) questions to
which *no* particular answer is "assumed" both by us all in ordinary
life & by the special sciences.

I do believe the division I mean does exist & is of great importance in considering the general conception of Philosophy: but
I ought to say at once that I don't think "assumed" is quite the
right word to use, either for the relation of (1) to us in ordinary
life, or for the different relation which I mean in the case of
scientists. I think "presupposed"—a word of which some philosophers are very fond—would express it better. But I don't
think there's *any* single word which will express what I mean.
I'm going to explain what I do mean; and the question I want
you to consider is whether this that I do mean isn't true, even
if it can't be properly expressed either by saying "assumed" or
"presupposed".

I'm going to treat "Reality as a whole" = "the Universe as a
whole" = "the World as a whole".

And I'll begin by giving 2 examples of questions, which seem
to me to be philosophical questions about Reality as a whole, to
which one particular answer is "presupposed", in the peculiar
sense I'm going to define, both by us all in ordinary life & by the
special sciences.

Consider these 2 props. (1) "Whatever else may be true about
the Universe, one thing that's true of it is that there have existed
in it in the past very large numbers of material things—material
things = "bodies" in the XVIII century sense—the sense in
which the moon is a body, my body is a body, this desk & blackboard are bodies". (2) "Whatever else may be true about the
Universe, it's true of it that very large numbers of changes have
occurred in it in the past".

I think both these props. may fairly be considered to be props.
about Reality as a whole. People who believe in them might say
"The existence of bodies is one fundamental feature of the
Universe", "The occurrence of change is one fundamental feature
of the Universe": meaning by "the existence of bodies" & "the
occurrence of change" nothing more, I think, than what I have
put down. The view being that any Universe in which there
are many material things must be very different from one in

which there are none; or any in which there are many changes from any in which there are none.

Well, then, these being props. about Reality as a whole, the question: Are they true? will in each case be a question about Reality as a whole. Only here the question asked is not strictly: Is it true that there have been many bodies or *not*? But is it true that there have been many, or *none* at all? and "Is it true that there have been many changes, or none at all?" It being, I think, for some reason always assumed when these questions are raised in philos. that, if there are any bodies, there are certainly many; if any changes, certainly many: so that the only alternatives it's necessary seriously to consider are: Are there many, or none at all?

It can't, I think, be denied that these questions have been discussed by philos., & if you discuss them *in certain sorts of ways*, but only in certain sorts of ways, you are doing philos.

We might say, it has been discussed: Is Matter real? Is change real?

And it seems to me that a particular answer to these questions, namely that there have been many material things, & there have been many changes, is "presupposed" by us all in ordinary life & the sciences in the following senses.

(1) *Ordinary Life.* That there have been many bodies is "presupposed" by us all in ordinary life, in the sense that we have all, in ordinary life, often *observed* facts from which, taken together, it strictly *follows* that there have been many bodies. For instance, I at this moment *observe* that there are a good many human bodies in this room, a good many desks, a good many articles of clothing, a blackboard. And I have very often in the past made similar observations. I've observed in walking down a street that there were a good many houses in it; in looking at a wood that there were a good many trees in it; in looking at a sea-beach that there were a great many pebbles on it. It seems not too much to say that *all* adult human beings have frequently observed facts of this sort: so that in the case of each of us, it follows from many facts that he has observed, taken together, that there have been large numbers of bodies in the Universe, whatever else may be true of it.

I am, of course, well aware, when I say this, of an objection which may occur to some of you at once. Many philosophers have

said that "observe" can be used in a sense such that it is not true
that, in that sense, I do observe that there are a good many human
bodies in this room, or that anyone ever has observed anything
of the sort. I think this is true: there is a sense of "observe", in
which philosophers sometimes use the word, & which is an
important notion about which we shall have to talk a great deal,
such that in *that* sense I don't observe that there are several
human bodies in this room, & never have observed [this].

Precisely the same applies to "No changes have ever taken
place". We have all often observed that so-&-so has moved; &
these facts, taken together, entail "Many changes have taken
place".

The props. "That many bodies have existed in the Universe"
& "that many changes have taken place in it" are therefore
entailed by things we have all *observed*.

(2) In the case of the special sciences, what I mean by saying
that these 2 props. are *presupposed* by them, is something different.
In their case I say they're entailed by *established conclusions* of
the sciences. One science, e.g., has established that thousands of
years ago there existed large numbers of enormous reptiles,
ichthyosauri & such like. This is a genuine conclusion of a science
& an established one; & from it there follows that there have been
many bodies in the Universe. Another science has established
that more than thousands of years ago just as now there were
millions of stars. This is a genuine conclusion of astronomy; &
from it again there follows that there have been many bodies in
the Universe.

And similarly of changes. That the earth has been very hot,
etc.

In discussing such questions about the nature of Reality as a
whole as "Is Matter real" & "Is change real", philosophers have
been discussing questions to which one particular answer, the
affirmative answer, follows both (a) from things we all observe
in ordinary life & (b) from established conclusions of many
sciences.

And I'm emphasising this because it seems to me to have a
very important bearing on the relation of philosophy to the
sciences; & therefore on the general conception of philosophy.

One thing that is very commonly aimed at in discussing what
philosophy is, is to give such a definition of it as will ensure that

no question discussed by philos. should be identical with any discussed by the sciences. It is felt that questions which fall within the province of some special science can't fall within that of philosophy. This for instance is very prominent in Broad. In insisting that it is the business of philos. to analyse such general concepts as cause, he points out, as necessary to defend himself, that none of the special sciences *do* analyse these very general concepts: he thinks they do analyse more special concepts, peculiar to themselves, e.g. physics the conception of mass; & that *therefore* the analysis of these doesn't belong to philosophy. And again no special science tries to discover whether every change has a cause. The idea is to allow to philos. only questions wh. don't belong to any particular science.

But now how about our questions: Is Matter Real? Is Change real?

It's true that no special sciences raise these abstract questions themselves; but if the sciences do raise & settle questions from which one particular answer to them *follows*, it seems to me obviously rather a subterfuge to say that in raising them it is raising questions which the scientists don't raise. For it is raising questions to which the sciences have *proved* that one particular answer is true, though they haven't said so; & raising questions such that, unless the philosopher answers them in one particular way, his answer will *conflict* with, be inconsistent with, the results of the sciences. And moreover if he does reach the same conclusion as the scientists, what's the use of his going over the ground again, & proving again what the scientists have already proved? It's admitted that it's not the business of philos. to discuss whether millions of stars existed a million years ago: that must be left to astronomy. But if so, how can it be his business to discuss whether it's true that many material things have existed in the Universe or none have? If he comes to the conclusion they have, he will be merely saying something which the astronomers have already proved; if he says none have, he will be contradicting the astronomers.

It seems to me that we can only allow these questions to belong to philos., if we insist that you will only be doing philos. if you discuss them *by a particular method*. And then the question arises whether the method used by the sciences isn't the best & the only proper method for settling such questions.

How is a philosopher to set about proving that there have been many material things in the Universe, or that there have been changes?

As for the way in which philosophers have reached the conclusion that Matter is not real, & Change is not real, I think something can be said about that. They have tried to shew that such props. as "There's a blackboard in this room" or "I moved my hand" are self-contradictory; & if they could shew this, no doubt that would prove their conclusion. You certainly are doing philosophy if you try to do that. And similarly you will be doing philos. if you try to shew that the arguments used by other phils. to shew this are invalid.

I've said some philosophers have denied that Matter is real: & at least one (McT.) certainly has.

Berkeley did not deny that Matter is real. All he did was to give a peculiar analysis of what's meant by saying it is. But here's the same sort of ambiguity as I pointed out, when I said I thought it doubtful whether anyone had ever been a Solipsist. What's expressed in this way may be merely a prop. of analysis.

Most questions which philosophers have raised about Reality as a whole seem to me to be of this nature. It's not easy to give questions which aren't except "God exists", "There are infinite attributes beside extension & thought".

(As for "Nothing is real but one single experience" it's not easy to say to which division it belongs.)

But people have a vague idea that something *could* be done in this way. That we might be able to discover all sorts of things about the Universe, not in conflict with what the sciences tell us about it, but supplementary to it.

Well, then, philosophers do raise these 2 kinds of questions about Reality as a whole (α) questions to which an answer is presupposed, (β) questions to which none is presupposed.

What *other* questions do they raise, besides those of analysis?

IV

OTHER PHILOSOPHICAL QUESTIONS

So far I've distinguished 2 main kinds of questions which it seems to me to be the business of philos. to discuss.

1. Questions about the meaning of particular words, phrases or forms of expression in common use (only *some*).

2. Questions about the nature of Reality as a whole—understood in a very wide & a very vague sense.

And I've divided questions which fall under 2, into two very different divisions

(α) questions about the world as a whole, to which one particular answer follows both from observations which we all make, & from established conclusions of the sciences (as instances of such questions I took: Do bodies exist = Is Matter real? And: Do changes occur?)

(β) questions about the world as a whole of which it is not true that any particular answer to them follows either from observations which we all make or from established conclusions of the sciences (as instances I gave (1) Does God exist? (2) Are there, as Spinoza said there were, an infinite number of "attributes" beside extension & thought).

I said I thought it was rather difficult to find examples of this kind of question, but I can give 2 others.

(A) Is it the case that, as Leibniz thought, this is the best of all possible worlds? You might think that one particular answer to this—the negative—follows from things which we have all observed; but I think it's plain it doesn't—it could only follow from things we observe together with an additional premiss—that certain kinds of things are bad—and this is not a thing we observe in the sense considered.

(B) My other example is Broad's: Is it true that every change has a cause? No answer to this follows from things we all observe, nor from any established conclusions of the sciences. (Even if, as B. says, it is true that, in some sense, we all always "assume" it in ordinary life, & all the sciences do too.)

But now do *all* the questions of philosophy fall under one or other of these 2 heads, (1) & (2)?

It would be very rash to say so: and there is one special kind of question, which ought, I think, to be mentioned in any general account of philosophy, though *perhaps* it falls under (2) or *partly* so.

Many philosophers have been very much interested in the question, with regard to particular *sorts* of propositions, whether any prop. of the *sort* in question is ever *known with certainty* to be true ⟨as distinguished from the question whether any such props. *are* true⟩: and I think it must be admitted that in the case of certain sorts, the question whether props. of that sort are ever known with certainty to be true is a philosophic question.

For instance: some philosophers have asked: do we ever know for certain, with regard to any prop. entailing that other people have experiences, that it is true? and others: do we ever know for certain with regard to any prop. entailing that a material thing exists, that it is true? and others: do we ever know with regard to any prop. entailing that so-&-so *was* the case (in the *past*), that it is true? These questions are often put in the form: Do we know with certainty of the existence of other people? Do we know with certainty of the existence of matter? Do we know with certainty that anything has existed in the past? But I want to emphasize that the real question is not, with regard to a single prop., e.g. "Other people have existed" or "Matter exists", whether we know *that* one to be true; but with regard to a whole *class* of props. in each case, from each of which these props. follow, whether we know any of *them* to be true. I think it would be admitted, & in any case I think it is true, that I certainly don't know for certain that other people have had experiences, unless I know the truth in particular cases of such props. as "This person is conscious now", "This person is seeing so-&-so", "This person is hearing so-&-so", "This person is thinking so-&-so", "This person is feeling so-&-so". And as I emphasized before, the question is always not: Do I know *at least one* such thing, or none? But: Do I know *many* or none? it being taken for granted that, if I know *one*, I certainly know many.

Now you will see at once how similar *some* questions of this sort are to questions which I've already classed as questions about reality as a whole. For instance, we now, instead of the question: Is Matter real?, have merely substituted the question: Do we *know* matter to be real? And it might be thought that, if we are to call the first a question about Reality as a whole, it must be fair to include the latter also. Indeed you can see that precisely the same answer might be an answer to both questions. To any question of the form: Is so-&-so the case? you may be giving a proper answer in each of 3 ways: viz. Yes, it is; No, it's not; or I don't know whether it is or not. And so to the question: Is Matter real, it *is* an answer to say: *We* don't know whether it is or not. And this, you see, is also an answer to the different question: Do we *know* whether Matter is real?

Take the case of the philosophical question: Does God exist? You all know that different people give to it each of the 3 answers: Yes; No; & we don't know whether he does or not. To believe the first people would say is called Theism; to believe the second is called Atheism; & to believe the 3rd Agnosticism. Agnosticism in this view is one possible answer to a question about Reality as a whole, namely Does God exist? But it is also at the same time an answer to the question: Do we *know* that God exists? Are we then to call this a question about Reality as a whole, or not?

I think we may fairly say that *in a sense* it is. And that similarly a question of the form: Do we know (that so-&-so is the case)? will always be in a sense a question about reality as a whole, if the so-&-so is such that the question: Is so-&-so the case? would be a question about Reality as a whole. And *most* philosophical questions of the form: Do we know that so-&-so is the case? do I think comply with this condition.

But nevertheless there is a very important difference between the question: Do we know that so-&-so is the case? & the question "Is so-&-so the case"?, where it is the same so-&-so that is in question.

Let me illustrate again by the familiar case of Theism, Atheism & Agnosticism. I think most people are apt to treat Theism & Agnosticism as mutually exclusive alternatives: if you are a Theist, it follows you're not an Agnostic; & if you're an Agnostic, it follows you're not a Theist. But if the def. I gave above of Agnosticism were the right one, it would follow that they are by no means incompatible; a man can be at the same time a Theist, & also an Agnostic—& perhaps in fact most Theists are also Agnostics. For we said a Theist is one who believes that God exists, an Agnostic one who believes that we don't know for certain whether he does or not. And obviously it's possible for a person to hold both views at once: indeed, I think perhaps most (certainly many) serious Theists do; they believe (sometimes very strongly) that God does exist, but at the same time they would deny that they or anyone knows for certain that he does; e.g. they say that the existence of God is not a matter of knowledge but of Faith. Similarly it's obviously perfectly possible for an Atheist to be also an Agnostic: he has only to believe that God does not exist, & also to believe that we don't know this for certain. This shews, I think, that the def. of Agnostic is not: one who believes that we don't know for certain; but one who does this, & *also* neither believes that he does *nor* that he doesn't; or perhaps believes that he doesn't & believes we don't know this for certain.

What I want to insist on is that you may give, & it is very common to give, a negative answer to the question: Do we know that Matter is real? & at the same time a positive one to the question: Is Matter real? Some philosophers have really held that Matter is not real; but many more have combined "we don't know that Matter is real", with a belief that it is. The *general* attitude has been: "Of course it *is* real, but we don't know for certain that it is".

Now I've said that in a sense: Do we know that Matter is real? Do we know for certain that God exists? are questions about Reality as a whole; but in a sense they're not. As you'll see they're questions about human knowledge; because what *"we"* means here is human beings who have lived on the earth, & *while* they had human bodies. The philosopher who asks these questions isn't asking: Do *any* human beings anywhere in the Universe (perhaps on Mars) know with certainty that God exists? Nor is he asking whether human beings, if they survive the death of their bodies, may not know it then? As you know, many religious people have held that human beings do survive the death of their bodies, & that then some of them do really *know* for certain of the existence of God—they see him face to face. If this were so, it would be true to say *some* human beings do *know* of God's existence. And *perhaps* this question is a philosophical question if treated in certain ways: it comes under Broad's head of questions about the *position & destiny of man*. But this is *not* the sort of question I'm now considering. When philosophers ask do *we* know, they always mean men, in human bodies, living on the earth: they mean do we know *in this life*. And so you see that, in

N

a way, this sort of question, so far from being a question about the Universe as a whole, is a question about a very limited part of the Universe; about a particular species of animals living on the earth, & asking a particular sort of thing about them—namely whether they *know* something, such that, if they did know it, they would be knowing something about the Universe as a whole. It seems to me certain that such kinds of questions, in spite of this limitation, must be reckoned as part of philosophy.

It would be quite a different question if it were asked: Is it possible for *any* being to know of the existence of God? or of the existence of Matter? To ask this would be to ask: Is it nonsense, or self-contradictory to say: Some being knows for certain of the existence of God or Matter. And it would come under our first head of questions of analysis (how difficult it is to distinguish clearly between questions of analysis & others): I'm not sure that the only good reasons for the opinion we *don't* know for certain, in both these cases, isn't that it's a sort of thing which it's inconceivable any being should know for certain. But this certainly *isn't* the only question which philosophers do in fact ask: they do in fact ask something about *us*, in this life. So that in asserting: *We* don't know, they are asserting: We exist, & therefore asserting the existence of matter.

Now I've said that in *most* of the cases where it is a philosophical question to ask: Do we know for *certain* that so &-so is the case? the so-&-so in question is such that the question: *Is* so-&-so the case? would be a question about Reality as a whole. But there is one particular class of cases where, if this is so at all, the question is a question about Reality as a whole in an entirely new sense, which I haven't yet distinguished.

It is a very remarkable & important fact, in considering philosophy, how many philosophers, when they have talked about knowledge or certainty & what sorts of props. we can know with certainty to be true, have referred to Mathematics & Formal Logic as giving instances of really certain knowledge—or knowledge as certain as we can get. They seem to think of $2 + 2 = 4$, & the Law of Contradiction, as giving instances of the kind of thing of which we can be really *certain*, if we can of anything. E.g. Russell in *Contemp. Philos.* (p. 359).[1] "I came to philos. through mathe-

---

[1] ["Logical Atomism". Reprinted in B. Russell, *Logic and Knowledge* (London, 1956).]

matics, or rather through the wish to find some reason to believe in the truth of mathematics. From early youth, I had an ardent desire to believe that there can be such a thing as knowledge, combined with a great difficulty in accepting much that passes as knowledge. It seemed clear that the *best chance of finding indubitable truth* would be in pure mathematics". R. seems here to say that he looked to philos. in the hope that through it he would be able to assure himself that some of the props. of pure mathematics were not merely true, but *indubitably* true (= known *by us* for certain to be true). That is to say he implies that in his view then the question: Are any of the props. of Pure Math. indubitably true? was a question which it is the business of philosophy to discuss. And he says nothing later to lead one to suppose that he has now changed his view as to whether this is a philos. question. He does not tell us what answer to this question he ultimately arrived at. He does tell us later that he thinks he discovered by his work on mathematical logical that mathematics *may* be true. But he adds that "to shew it *is* true would require other methods & other considerations", & he does not tell us whether he has found any; still less whether he has found any to shew it is *indubitably true.* (N.B. he seems to imply that it is the business of philos. to discuss whether math. is true; thus raising the same sort of puzzling question as to the relation of philos. to math., wh. I said was raised by the fact that philosophers do raise questions to which the sciences imply an answer. Surely it's the business of the mathematicians to decide whether particular mathematical props. are true? And if so what's the use of the philosopher discussing whether *any* math. props. are true? Suppose he decides they are, can he give better reasons than the mathematicians give? Suppose he decides they aren't. He's contradicting the mathematicians. And aren't they better judges? It's admitted not to be the business of philos. to discuss whether particular *theorems* are true. But, if he insists on discussing whether *any* are, he's bound either to contradict the maths., or to be doing something wh. seems superfluous.)

Now I think we must regard the question whether math. props. are *certain*, are known to be true, as a philosophical question. But, if so, is *that* a question about Reality as a whole? Only, if at all, in a very different sense from that in which: Does God exist? Does Matter exist? Does Change exist? are so. It might be

N*

said that $2 + 2 = 4$ is a prop. about Reality as a whole—bec. it is universal. But what "question about Reality as a whole" naturally means is what sorts of *contingent* props. are true—things which might have been otherwise. But $2 + 2 = 4$, & $\sim(p . \sim p)$ are totally different sorts of props.: if true at all, they are things which couldn't have been otherwise. In Leibniz's language, they are necessary truths, things which must have been true in any possible world; & therefore give us no information as to *this* world: whereas to ask about Reality as a whole is to ask what sort of a world this world is.

I think, therefore, so far as philos. discusses whether any math. & logical props. are known *with certainty* to be true, it can't properly be said to be discussing a question about Reality as a whole, even in the modified sense in which in discussing "Do we know that God exists?" we are doing so.

But now there's one other question about human knowledge which has certainly been discussed by some philosophers, & which must, I think, be admitted to belong to philos. I've said it's always philosophy to discuss: Do we know that so-&-so is the case? where "Is so-&-so the case?" is a philosophic question; & that this (except in the case of Maths.) may be so only where the latter is a question about Reality as a whole.

But now some philosophers have not contented themselves with discussing isolated questions of this sort; but have tried to arrive at true props. of the form: Props. of the sorts A or B, or the sort C, are the *only* sorts of props. we know with certainty to be true. In other words: What sorts of props. (if any) do we, human beings living in bodies on the earth, know with certainty to be true? This, if it is assumed that we do know *some*, is the question as to the *limits of human knowledge*, prominent in Locke & Kant.

In answer to this question, some have given (in words at all events) the answer: (1) Nothing is certain—which is called Absolute Scepticism; others (2) Nobody ever knows any props. to be true for certain except props. about his own present experience at the moment in question—Epistemological Solipsism of the present moment; [yet others] (3) Nobody knows any except props. asserting something about his own present & past experience.

(There's one other thing I want to notice: namely that assertions to the effect [that] nothing of this sort is *certain* are liable to conflict with results of the sciences. The sciences will say: This is certain. Is the philosopher a better judge than the scientist?)

It is a sort of question wh. has been very prominent in philos.: What are the limits of Human knowledge? It is why Locke, Berkeley, Hume, Kant called their books, books about the Human Understanding, Principles of Human Knowledge, Critique of Pure Reason (= man's reason). All of them were, I think, trying to answer more or less clearly this kind of question.

And I want to illustrate by kinds of answers that have been given to it. Various forms of Scepticism are the most prominent, bec. they limit human knowledge most.

(1) Absolute Scepticism. No human being ever knows anything for certain. Some philos. have *said* this; but others have said that it is nonsense—you can't mean anything by it. That all you can say with meaning is: Mentioning a certain type, we know *none* of that type.

(2) The next most extreme form would be one wh. so far as I know doesn't exist: it would be a philosopher taking one single prop. & saying *that* is the only prop. that anyone ever knew for certain. I can imagine things wh. might tempt a philosopher to say this: e.g. "God exists", "I exist".

It's an important thing that the general view has been that, if we know *anything* for certain, we know *several* things.

I said that besides questions of the form: Do we know for certain that so-&-so is the case? it seemed to me also that it is the business of philos. to try to answer questions of the form: Have we any reason to believe that so-&-so is the case? I think you will find that philosophers have been very much occupied with discussing questions of this form; and I don't think it can be denied that when you discuss certain questions of this form, in a certain way, you are doing philosophy.

But in the case of *what* sort of props., or classes of props., is it a philosophical question to ask: Have we any reason to believe that this prop. is true or that any props. of this class are true? Obviously not in the case of *all*; and so far as I can see the props. & classes of props. with regard to which it is philos. to ask this are precisely the same as those with regard to wh. it is philos. to ask: Do we know for certain that this prop. is true, or that any props. of this class are true?

E.g. if you've decided: We don't know for certain that God exists, it will be proper to go on to ask: Have we any reason to believe that God exists? (though not, if you decide: We *do* know for certain); & if you've decided: We don't know for certain any props. which entail the existence of material things, or any mathem. props., it will be proper to ask: Have we any reason to believe any?

But now it might be thought that the question: Have we any reason to believe that matter exists? can hardly be distinguished from the question: Does matter exist?

But I think it ought to be distinguished; & that the view that there's no difference between them is due to overlooking a distinction which philosophers do very often overlook: viz. the distinction between the question I ask when I ask: Have *I* any reason to believe . . .? & the question: Have *we* any reason to believe . . .?

So far as I can see there *is* no important difference between: Does matter exist? &: Have *I* any reason to believe that it does?, when *I* ask both. If I start discussing the first, having settled that I don't know it for certain, I shall certainly discuss whether I have any reasons for it; & shall conclude that it does only if I believe I have *more* reason to believe that it does than that it doesn't.

(N.B. "Have I, or we, any reason to believe?" may, strictly, mean either of 2 things. One meaning of: Have I any reason for p ? is: Do I know anything which is evidence for, or an argument in favour of p; and as you all know, it may be the case that there is *some* evidence for p, & yet *more* evidence for not-p. In a detective story some facts may favour the hypothesis that A committed the murder, others that B. There is *some* reason to believe each. Generally in philos. what is meant by: Have we *any* reason to believe p, is, I think, "Have we *more* reason to believe p than not-p". But you can also ask: Have we any reason at all? E.g. McT. concluded with regard to matter that we haven't any reason *at all* to believe in its existence.)

But why is there an important difference between "have I?" & "have *we*?". As you all know, *I* may have good reason to believe a thing, which it's *not* true that we all have reason to believe. To say we *all* have is to say something immensely more than that *I* have. But in the case of philosophical questions it is I think always assumed, curiously enough, that if *I* have no reason to believe that God exists, neither has anybody else; & if *I* have, then everybody has. This is an assumption which *needs* to be justified.

Now I said that in the case of human knowledge, philosophers have tried & it is their business to try (1) to give an exhaustive list of *kinds* of props. we know for certain, (2) in the case of any kind, with regard to wh. they conclude we *do* know, to raise the question: *How* do we know?, & I *might* have added (3) attempt to give an exhaustive list of the *ways* in which we know things.

All this holds, *mutatis mutandis*, of *have reason to believe*: (1) you can attempt to give an exhaustive list of the *kinds* of props. we have reason to believe, (2) you can raise the question: *What* reason have we to believe so-&-so?, & (3) attempt to give an exhaustive list of the *kinds* of reason which are good reasons for believing anything.

Also, just as with knowledge, philosophers in discussing: Have we any good reason for believing props. of such-&-such a sort? are liable to come into conflict with the sciences; so with: have we reason to believe? For the sciences *do* say not only p, & p is certain, but there's *good evidence for* p: & it has happened that p belongs to a class of props. with regard to wh. philosophers have concluded: We *never* have good evidence for a prop. of that sort. Isn't the fact that the sciences say: Such-&-such *is* good evidence for so-&-so, a reason for saying: It *is* good evidence?

But there's one extra question connected with "have reason for", which doesn't arise with regard to knowledge, taken strictly. I said: Have we reason to believe p, often means Have we more reason to believe p than not-p. And we can of course ask also: Have we *more* reason to believe p than q? This sort of question with regard to different classes of props., of the sort with regard to wh. it is the business of philos. to discuss: Have we reason to believe them?, is often raised by philosophers & seems to me certainly to belong to philosophy. I, e.g., should say that we have *more* reason to believe that matter exists than to believe that other people believe that matter exists: bec. in saying the latter, you are already saying that matter exists, & also something more: it's *more* certain that matter exists than that *we* believe. Other philosophers have often said the contrary: they often say it's quite certain we believe it; & not quite certain that it does exist

—which is absurd. Similarly I said that it's *as* certain that other people *observe* facts about material objects as that they believe props. about them. So again a theist, who hold that there's much more reason to believe that God exists than that he doesn't, may nevertheless hold that the existence of Matter is more *certain* than that of God. This type of question as to the order of reasonableness or certainty seems to me quite certainly to belong to philos.

To sum up. (1) Questions about the meaning of words, phrases & forms of expression: Analysis, (2) Questions about Reality as a whole, (3) A number of questions about human knowledge, (4) Still more questions about what it's *reasonable for us to believe* & *in what degree*.

I don't see how it can be denied that *all* these sorts of questions do belong to philos. Of course, people may say that they *oughtn't* to: but as philos. is now used they *do*.

But now I want to return for a moment to the omitted part of Broad's description of Speculative Phil.: philos. is expected to consider the position & prospects of men in the Universe.

Now the questions: What sorts of things do we *know* about it? What sorts of things have we reason to believe about it? may by a stretch be said to be questions about the position of men in it. And these I have said do belong to philos.

But what other *questions* about man's position in it are philos.? & what about his prospects?

Nobody would say the question whether life is likely to cease on this earth is philos.: that is a question for science.

I can only think of the future life & immortality.

These aren't questions discussed by any *actual* science. But aren't they questions, which, if answerable at all, are answerable by the methods of science?

Only not if you try to settle it by *a priori* arguments, such as for instance (1) a thing can be destroyed only by division, (2) the soul is indivisible. That style of arg. *is* philos., but I should say bad philos.

Does this exhaust the kind of questions which are philosophical? Prob. not; but I do think I've mentioned *most* of the kinds. I can't think of any important exception.

V

PHILOSOPHICAL METHODS

It seems to me there is nothing wh. can be described as *the* method of philos. There can't be if it deals both with questions of analysis & with the other sort of questions.

Methods of analysis. I doubt if there's any *one* method. How did R. discover his prop. about def. descriptions?

You look for other props. which are *necessary conditions* of its truth, i.e. props. such that it can't be true, unless they are true; it must be false if they are false. And he found first 2 such: Somebody wrote W.; Not more than one person did, i.e. it wasn't a work of joint authorship like Beaumont & Fletcher. These 2 are necessary for the truth. This at once gives a *partial* analysis.

These things he concludes must be part of what you're asserting.

But they're not the whole. They're not *sufficient.* They're sufficient for "The author of Wav. was a real person". What else can you find?

It's obviously also necessary that, if you met a person of whom the 2 things were true, it should also be true of him that he was a Scotsman.

⟨But if you ask: How do you know that it does entail this?, the answer is your general knowledge of the English language. Only here again there's a method wh. consists in looking about for *instances.* E.g. "have the same parents" and then it occurs to you that a person may be only a half-brother. A method of shewing that so-&-so is *not* necess. or *not* sufficient.⟩

You would have proved it true (verified it) if you had found all this to be the case; & you would have found it *false* if you'd found any part of what it asserts *not* to be the case.

Obviously then in a sense you've discovered what it means, if you've discovered what would *verify* it & all the things that would *prove* it false.

And this is different from saying that's what you were *thinking of* when you *said it.*

But the meaning of verify is here quite different than in: finding that the pavements have been wet verifies (proves) that

191

it has been raining. It doesn't *follow* from their being wet that it has been raining; nor from that it has been raining that they will be wet.

It is, it seems to me, often one of the most difficult things about analysis to be sure whether a prop. q which is such that it *proves* p, proves it logically or only by experience.

I was talking about what rules can be given in answer to the question: How am I to set about finding an analytic def. of a word or phrase or expression?

And I said I thought this was one good rule:

(1) Take a prop., p, in the expression of which your phrase occurs & look about to see if you can find any other sentences in which your phrase doesn't occur which express props. that are necessary but not sufficient conditions for the truth of p: = props. which follow from p, but from which p doesn't follow.

Thus R. found that 2 necess. conditions for the truth of

"The author of W. was Scotch" are

"At least one person wrote W."

"Not more than one wrote W."

(2) Having found as many as you can, go on to consider if you can find an expression in which these necessary conditions are expressly mentioned, & which is such that *both* it follows from p (is a necess. condit.) & p follows from it (is a sufficient condition).

You see that p says something more than "q & r", & you try to find an expression which expressly says q & r & something more, wh. satisfies these conditions.

How you're to do this I can give *no* rule: you just simply have to try to think of more. I only said you mustn't assume that it will be of the form q & r & s.

I said all that this can end in is giving you another—*more analysed*—sentence such that you can say this prop. entails & is entailed by your original one.

But I emphasized that where you can say p entails q, & q entails p, it doesn't seem to be always true that q is what you were *thinking* when you thought p: & that where p entails q but *not* vice versa, it doesn't seem always true that in thinking that p you were thinking that q.

I said I thought that for the purposes of philos. it doesn't matter what the answer is to the question: What was I thinking when I thought p? If you've discovered a more analysed expression, expressing a prop. which entails & is entailed by p, you've done all a philosopher need want to do. I still think this is so, but I don't know.

It *is* a question for philos. what this "thinking of" consists in, because it's a question what "meaning" means; but I think you've done the important part of analysis, if you've done the other.

Now I want to go on to the question: Supposing you've thought of a q, which you think satisfies this condition, or another philos. offers one to you: how are you to *test* whether it's true or not?

This, you will see, is merely the question: How are you to tell whether p does entail q?

Now here in *some* cases it seems to be sufficient just to know the language: so soon as you understand how the word "mother" is used & how the word "female" is used, you can see that

x was mother of y . entails . x was female.

But often p does entail q, when you can't just see that it does: in Math. or *Princ. Math.* you *deduce* q from p; you only *have* deduced q from p, if q follows from p, and a proof wouldn't be necess. if you could just see that it did follow.

Thus it would be possible to *prove* that "Whoever wrote Wav. was Scotch" + the other 2 entails "The author . . ." & vice versa.

What methods are there for answering questions about reality as a whole?

Here I'll take particular examples, one of each class of question; of the first class: Is Matter real? of the second: Does God exist? though probably this isn't sufficient.

What method is there for discussing whether Matter is real or not?

I think it's useful here to distinguish between the question: What methods *have been* used? & What methods ought to be used?

If you take this question seriously you want to ask: Are there any good reasons (conclusive, if possible) for believing it doesn't exist? Are there any good reasons (conclusive, if possible) for thinking it does?

And so far as I know 2 methods have been used to prove that

matter *doesn't*: i.e. it has been supposed that 2 kinds of conclusive reasons can be given for the conclusions that it doesn't.

1. It has been supposed possible to shew that every prop. which entails the existence of a material object is self-contradictory; e.g. "There's a blackboard in this room now".

Now this method, if successful, certainly would prove its point.

Ought you to look to see whether it does? I think, since so many philosophers of the first rank have believed this, it is one of the businesses of philosophy to examine their arguments. And such investigation generally has *indirect* results in clearing up the meaning of expressions.

I think the result is that they're *not* self-contradictory; but I see no way of proving that they can't be.

2. McT.'s method of trying to prove: Nothing can be real but what has such-&-such characteristics; matter hasn't got them; therefore matter isn't real. Perhaps Hegel had the same.

This also, if successful, would be a good method: and I think the same remarks apply to it.

But now supposing you can't find any good reasons for saying it doesn't: can you find any for saying it does?

1. Here a method has been used by Descartes, in which one of the premises is the existence of God & veracity of God.

I do not think this is successful; because I don't think there is any good reason for thinking that God exists.

But I suppose this sort of argument *ought* to be investigated.

2. I've insisted the sciences give indirect proofs of this, by proving that particular material things have existed: I instanced the proof of the existence of Plesiosauri, Ichthyosauri, etc.; & of the existence of millions of stars 10,000 years ago.

Now these props. are not philosophic props. And I want to give one reason why I think they are not. All scientific proofs of the existence of particular kinds of material things seem to me to assume as premisses the existence of others: the proof of ichthyosauri assumes the existence of fossils; that of stars 10,000 years ago the existence of stars *now*.

Relation to logic, psychology and ethics.

(1) *Logic*. I think the chief thing here to be said is that the word "Logic" is used in two very different senses; & the relation of philosophy to each of the 2 is quite different.

(a) Sometimes by *logic* is meant simply the working out of a formal system: such as e.g. the formal theory of the syllogism or that of *Principia Mathematica*. Here the sort of thing you are told is that from certain premisses certain conclusions *follow*: e.g. that from All S is P, A is S, A is P *follows*; *or* All S is P All M are S, All M are P. Or any of the *proofs* in *Princ. Math.*

This subject is not philosophy at all; any more than mathematics is.

(b) People talk of logic as the analysis of thinking ⟨the morphology of knowledge⟩; & include in it such questions as what "true" & "false" mean, what is a proposition, what does "follow from" mean, what *is* a class?

These simply are questions of Critical Philosophy, the part dealing with analysis. They're just a *part* of it.

But also in logic, espec. Inductive logic, it seems to me there certainly are often included questions of the sort: *What is a good reason for believing what?* I.e. the general question: What conditions must be fulfilled by props. (or sets of props.) p & q in order that, if a person knows p, he may be said to have good reason for believing q?

Which *may* be a question of analysis.

(2) *Psychology*. Here, too, we have to say that 2 different subjects are included in Psych., which have very different relations to philosophy. One part is just a *part* of philosophy; the other is a science that has no more to do with philosophy than physics or chemistry or biology.

(a) The *science* of psychology, the object of which is to discover, by observation & experiment, laws with regard to *mental* facts, either mere generalisations *or* causal laws.

Take such a book as Prof. Bartlett's on Remembering. He conducted a number of experiments; made generalisations; & suggestions as to the cause of the observed results.

(b) Other psychology books often include, along with material of this kind, analyses such as James' "The present thought is the only thinker". This kind of psychology is again simply a department of philos.: the analytic part.

But you see this is *not* analysis of concepts which occur in *all* sciences; but only in ordinary life & in Psych. I think we have to *add* to analysis as defined by Broad the analysis of concepts *only* occurring in special sciences.

It is, I think, bec. both these 2 different kinds of things occur both in Logic & in Psych., that it is supposed that these are more closely related to Philos.

(3) *Ethics.* Is it distinguished from Moral Philosophy?

If not, it's just a sub-division of philos., which I ought perhaps to have mentioned as such.

Partly analysis of what's meant by "good", "ought", "right", "wrong", "valuable", etc.

And *if* certain analyses of these are right, then *other* ethical props., ones which aren't analytic, wouldn't be philosophical at all, but belong to Psych., Sociology, or the theory of Evolution.

If naturalistic analyses are wrong, then it seems to me some other props. do belong to philos.: e.g. Pleasure is not the only good.

INDEX OF PROPER NAMES

MUIRHEAD LIBRARY OF PHILOSOPHY

An admirable statement of the aims of the Library of Philosophy was provided by the first editor, the late Professor J. H. Muirhead, in his description of the original programme printed in Erdmann's *History of Philosophy* under the date 1890. This was slightly modified in subsequent volumes to take the form of the following statement:

'The Muirhead Library of Philosophy was designed as a contribution to the History of Modern Philosophy under the heads: first of Different Schools of Thought—Sensationalist, Realist, Idealist, Intuitivist; secondly of different Subjects—Psychology, Ethics, Political Philosophy, Theology. While much had been done in England in tracing the course of evolution in nature, history, economics, morals and religion, little had been done in tracing the development of thought on these subjects. Yet "the evolution of opinion is part of the whole evolution".

'By the co-operation of different writers in carrying out this plan it was hoped that a thoroughness and completeness of treatment, otherwise unattainable, might be secured. It was believed also that from writers mainly British and American fuller consideration of English Philosophy than it had hitherto received might be looked for. In the earlier series of books containing, among others, Bosanquet's *History of Aesthetic*, Pfleiderer's *Rational Theology since Kant*, Albee's *History of English Utilitarianism*, Bonar's *Philosophy and Political Economy*, Brett's *History of Psychology*, Ritchie's *Natural Rights*, these objects were to a large extent effected.

'In the meantime original work of a high order was being produced both in England and America by such writers as Bradley, Stout, Bertrand Russell, Baldwin, Urban, Montague, and others, and a new interest in foreign works, German, French and Italian, which had either become classical or were attracting public attention, had developed. The scope of the Library thus became extended into something more international, and it is entering on the fifth decade of its existence in the hope that it may contribute to that mutual understanding between countries which is so pressing a need of the present time.'

The need which Professor Muirhead stressed is no less pressing today, and few will deny that philosophy has much to do with enabling us to meet it, although no one, least of all Muirhead himself, would regard that as the sole, or even the main, object of philosophy. As Professor Muirhead continues to lend the distinction of his name to the Library of Philosophy it seemed not inappropriate to allow him to recall us to these aims in his own words. The emphasis on the history of thought also seemed to me very timely; and the number of important works promised for the Library in the very near future augur well for the continued fulfilment, in this and other ways, of the expectations of the original editor.

H. D. LEWIS